The Junior League of Denver

PRESENTS

Centennial

Celebrations

A COLORADO COOKBOOK

Photography by Briana Marie

JUNIOR LEAGUE OF DENVER, INC.
1140 Delaware Street
Denver, CO 80204
Phone 303-692-0270
jld.org

This cookbook is a collection of favorite recipes, which are not necessarily original recipes.

JLD History taken from Ellen Kingman Fisher's book *Junior League of Denver: Leaders in Community Service, 1918–1993,* published by the Colorado Historical Society in 1993.

ISBN: 978-0-9603946-9-2
Library of Congress Catalog Number: 2019931879

Printed in China
10 9 8 7 6 5 4 3 2 1

Centennial Celebrations was edited, designed, and manufactured by Favorite Recipes Press in collaboration with Junior League of Denver. Favorite Recipes Press works with top chefs, food and appliance manufacturers, restaurants and resorts, health organizations, Junior Leagues, and nonprofit organizations to create award-winning cookbooks and other food-related products. Favorite Recipes Press is an imprint of Southwestern Publishing Group, Inc., 2451 Atrium Way, Nashville, Tennessee 37214. Southwestern Publishing Group is a wholly owned subsidiary of Southwestern/Great American, Inc., Nashville, Tennessee.

Christopher G. Capen, President,
    Southwestern Publishing Group
Sheila Thomas, President and Publisher,
    Favorite Recipes Press
Shelly Peppel, Designer
Steve Newman, Production Designer
Kristin Connelly, Managing Editor
Linda Brock, Editor
Rhonda Brock, Proofreader
frpbooks.com | 800-358-0560

For more information about where to purchase the Junior League of Denver's complete collection of award-winning cookbooks, please visit jld.org.

Colorado Cache, 1978
Crème de Colorado, 1987
Colorado Collage, 1995
Colorado Colore, 2002
Colorado Classique, 2009

MISSION

The Junior League of Denver, Incorporated, founded in 1918, is an organization of women committed to promoting voluntarism, developing the potential of women, and improving communities through the effective action and leadership of trained volunteers. Its purpose is exclusively educational and charitable.

WHO WE ARE

The Junior League of Denver (JLD) is a women's training organization that develops civic leaders committed to improving our community. We are currently working to improve literacy rates and provide access to books for children through the third grade. Over the past one hundred years, the League started, and aided in starting, many well-known Denver institutions, including Children's Museum of Denver, Mile High Transplant Bank, the Red Rocks concerts, and many others.

FOUNDATION

The Junior League of Denver Foundation was incorporated in 1992 with the sole purpose of sustaining the Junior League of Denver. Yearly distributions from the JLD Foundation support the mission and programs of the JLD, as designated by the JLD Board of Directors. The JLD Foundation represents a long-term development strategy to assure the continued vitality of the JLD in its mission of promoting voluntarism, contributing to the community, and training women leaders.

Proceeds from *Centennial Celebrations* support the mission and community focus of the Junior League of Denver, Inc.

Page 275

Page 51

Page 229

Page 117

Page 264

Page 84

Page 208

Page 141

Contents

Professional Credits

BRIANA MARIE—PHOTOGRAPHER

brianamarie.com

Briana has been a successful photographer in Napa Valley for eleven years, covering the rich stories of the people and places that make her native region so alive. Her local work quickly and organically grew to include cookbooks, publications, and commercial work for top organizations around the world.

Briana's work reflects the sensitive nature in which she approaches life and her subjects and the joy she finds in photography. She artfully captures intimate details and illuminates the essence of an ordinary day. Her greatest joy and challenge is to find beauty wherever she lands. Her uncompromising search for amazing light and goodness has led her to exquisite locations around the world, photographing food and wine, lifestyle portraits, fabulous events, and worthy nonprofits. Briana has been published in *National Geographic Travel, Wine Spectator, Harper's Bizarre, Forbes, Haute Living, Style Me Pretty, People Magazine, Bicycling Magazine, Grace Ormonde, Home & Design, San Francisco Chronicle, Decanter,* and *The Somm Journal.*

Her studio is nestled among the hills in Napa Valley, California, where she surrounds herself with farms, food, artists, and animals. When she's not slinging cameras, she can be found adventuring with her husband and two boys.

SALLY JAMES—CHEF

chefsroll.com/SallyJames

Sally James is an award-winning Australian author, educator, chef, stylist, and presenter, whose books and recipes have won international acclaim for food and wine pairing, health, and creativity. She is the author of eighteen cookbooks and publications, two of which won international awards.

Since relocating to the US in 2001, James has been a guest presenter on *Food Network* and *UPN* and has been featured in magazines including *Cooking Light, Wine Spectator, Fitness, Family Circle, New York Times' Savor Wine Country, Plate,* and *Healthy Cooking.* She has also been a guest chef and lecturer for the American Heart Association, the Culinary Institute of America, Disney's Epcot International Food & Wine Festival, COPIA, Aspen Food and Wine Classic, the National Restaurant Association Show, Draegar's and Publix Markets, the American Institute of Food & Wine, and Johnson & Wales Universities across the United States. She has always enjoyed creating and styling dishes that are as visually appealing as they are delicious, and selecting plateware and props that enhance the appeal. Her motto is "You first eat with your eyes, and the palate follows. It is the eyes that set the experience."

ERIN HORNSTEIN—FLORAL DESIGNER

plumsageflowers.com

After years of working in flower shops in Boulder and Chicago and on an organic farm in Boulder, owner Erin Hornstein was asked by several customers and friends to create wedding flowers. Her fresh and creative vision led to the creation of Plum Sage Flowers in the spring of 2005. By word of mouth, she began creating fabulous flowers for numerous weddings and special events. Plum Sage now resides in a design studio in a late 1800s home in the West Wash Park neighborhood of Denver, with a crew of flower enthusiasts and studio pups. Plum Sage creates stunning flower arrangements for weddings, holidays, special events, and weekly or everyday occasions. Plum Sage prefers to purchase locally grown, organic product and buys locally during the summer months to support Colorado farmers.

Nicole Cruse—Event Planner

graceandgatherevents.com

I'm Nicole, founder of Grace & Gather Events, and I'm a gathering planner. I believe celebrations in life are essential. When we think about events, we tend to think about the ingredients of an event: the mechanics, the logistics, and, of course, the pretty stuff. While these things are important, I believe a great gathering has more.

As a planner, I get that when there's a "why" behind your event, it isn't just for show. It's about creating an elevated way for those who love and support you to celebrate life's moments along with you. I also believe connecting with the right vendors is fundamental, because when there's a perfect match between you and your vendors, your unique event comes together like magic.

I've planned over forty gatherings—from weddings to showers to style shoots. What keeps me going? Taking care of every detail—so you can be fully present at your special event. I'd love to help you plan your next gathering.

Patricia Bainter—Creative Consultant

thepatricianpalette.com

Patricia Bainter earned the coveted Le Grand Diplôme® from Le Corden Bleu, London. She uses her culinary training and restaurant experience to write about food, develop recipes, style food for photography, design kitchens from a chef's perspective, and produce artful culinary canvases. She worked on the *Centennial Celebrations* Committee as Sustaining Cookbook Advisor and *Colorado Classique* as Sponsorship Chair and has been actively involved in the Junior League since 1997. She can be found at her website, where her goal is to entertain, teach, inspire, and create food worth framing.

Event Rents

eventrents.net

Event Rents is Colorado's premier party rental provider. Our exceptional client service, quality products, and attention to detail are the components that have made us the superior choice in the event rental industry. We are committed to providing our clients a first-rate level of expertise, service, and responsiveness. We are a steady resource so that our clients can focus their energy on the special event at hand. Simply, we do our job so that your special event is just that—special.

Yonder House

houseofyonder.com

Yonder House offers a curated collection of beautiful decor, wild floral designs, and custom design creations to accent your wedding or special event. Our team of Yonderettes works tirelessly from the conceptual design phase to the event day installations to assure that your day is simply magical and totally, uniquely you. From stylish tableware offerings to custom event statement installations, our team can create anything imaginable to bring your dreams to fruition. At Yonder House, you truly feel like you are home amongst those that don't accept the status quo.

Cookbook Committees

Cookbook Chair

Mary Beth McErlane

Sustaining Advisors

Cookbook Advisor

Patricia Bainter

Subcommittee Advisors

Corinne Ablin

Kristin Brownson

Cissie Megyesy Busch

Caroline Gash

Lynne Siegel

Laura Stenovec

Design and Editing

Chairs

Wendy Cutler Lowe

Stacey Rubinstein

Committee

Grace Devlin Bird

Kimberly Eckert

Tess Enright

Laurel Walk

Recipe Collection and Testing

Chairs

Christine Dupont-Patz

Ashley Moery Keski

Committee

Sean Maddox Cameron

Aubrey Coggins

Alicia Harrell George

Katie Lindsay Harmon

Katie Henry

Jenny Rementer

Jennifer Rich

Nell Roberts

Kibby Wilson

Tonia DeGregory Wilson

Sales and Marketing

CHAIRS

Alana Hancock   Sandy Hazzard

COMMITTEE

Teresa Blount   Megan Hannen   Katie Mata

Sponsorship

CHAIR

Hannah Strunc

COMMITTEE

Chrissy Fedorowicz   Michelle Grappo   Kimberly Vestal

JLD Staff

FINANCE & OPERATIONS DIRECTOR

Karen Bergen Mayo

COMMUNICATIONS DIRECTOR

Vanessa Banker

DEVELOPMENT COORDINATOR

Lesley Gibson

BUSINESS SUPPORT SPECIALIST

Celeste Sims

2016 & 2017 Feasibility Committees

Lora Adams	Anna Diemoz	Allison Ingalls	Alyssa Russo
Angela Andrews	Annie Douden	Ali Kaiser	Becky Schaub
Betsy Armstrong	Tess Enright	Isabelle Pearson	Brittany Sever
Kate Cihon	Erin Haucke	Lucy Robertson	Carrie Veatch
Lauren O'Neill Crist-Fulk	Angela Hooper	Stacey Rubinstein	Laurel Walk

A Centennial Celebration

Introduction

The Junior League of Denver was founded in 1918 with the knowledge that when a woman shares her gifts, she can accomplish great things. Whether those gifts come from their tables or their hearts, the women of JLD have served the communities of the Centennial State with grace and determination for more than one hundred years. Throughout the past century, Denver has transformed into a city where urban sophistication meets outdoor adventure, but many traditions stay the same. Food still has the power to unite people, and the everyday celebrations that surround good food are always the most memorable.

The sixth cookbook in JLD's award-winning collection, *Centennial Celebrations* includes more than 200 thoughtfully selected and thoroughly tested recipes, perfect for every season and occasion—from crowd-pleasing game day appetizers and traditional holiday favorites to light summer fare and winter comfort foods. *Centennial Celebrations* is a journey of the senses, featuring beautiful photography of fabulous gatherings at iconic Denver locations. The creative menus, recipes, and entertaining tips will inspire you to cook, connect, and celebrate . . . Colorado style!

Appetizers & Beverages

Menu
Gatherings To Go

SPRING

Watermelon Rosé Margaritas ~ 53

Blood Orange Cocktail ~ 51

Picnic Skewers ~ 31

Summer-Style Orzo Salad ~ 131

Peach Cupcakes with Brown Sugar Frosting ~ 255

Let's Rock

In 1947, the Junior League of Denver, along with the May Company, sponsored the first-ever concert series at the now world-famous Red Rocks Park and Amphitheatre. Since then, Red Rocks has hosted everything from symphonies and rock bands to operas and rap performances. Over the years, it also has become a place to exercise, worship, watch iconic films, or just stand in awe of this naturally formed outdoor venue. Every spring, summer, and fall, locals and visitors arrive early for their favorite shows so they can tailgate and soak in the mesmerizing views of Red Rocks.

Caramelized Garlic Tart

SERVES 6 TO 8

1 (13-ounce) puff pastry sheet, thawed
Cloves of 3 medium heads garlic (about 40 cloves)
1 tablespoon extra-virgin olive oil
1 cup water
1 tablespoon balsamic vinegar
¾ tablespoon sugar
1 teaspoon chopped fresh rosemary
1 teaspoon chopped fresh thyme

4 ½ ounces chive and onion cream cheese spread, chopped
4 ½ ounces smoked Gouda cheese, chopped
2 eggs
6 ½ tablespoons heavy cream
6 ½ tablespoons crème fraîche
½ teaspoon salt, or to taste
½ teaspoon black pepper, or to taste

Roll the pastry on a lightly floured surface. Fit the pastry into a shallow 11-inch fluted tart pan with a removable bottom; trim the edge. Cover with an 11-inch circle of parchment paper and arrange pie weights on the paper. Chill for 20 minutes.

Preheat the oven to 350 degrees.

Bake the pastry for 20 minutes. Remove the weights and paper carefully. Bake the pastry for 20 to 25 minutes longer or until golden brown. Reduce the oven temperature to 325 degrees.

Meanwhile, combine the garlic and enough water to cover in a small saucepan. Bring to a simmer. Cook for 3 minutes; drain well. Dry the saucepan and return to the heat. Cook the garlic in the olive oil in the saucepan over high heat for 2 minutes. Add 1 cup water and the balsamic vinegar. Bring to a boil. Simmer over medium heat for 10 minutes. Add the sugar, rosemary and thyme. Simmer for 30 minutes or until most of the liquid has evaporated and the garlic is coated with dark caramel syrup.

Sprinkle the cream cheese and Gouda cheese in the tart crust. Spoon the garlic mixture evenly over the cheese. Whisk the eggs, heavy cream, crème fraîche, salt and pepper in a small bowl. Pour evenly over the garlic mixture. Bake for 35 to 45 minutes or until the filling is set and golden brown. Remove the side of the pan. Garnish with thyme sprigs and serve warm.

Irish Nachos with Cider–Braised Onions

The National Onion Association tells the story of the bulb onion, promoting the usage and visibility of the third most-consumed fresh vegetable in the US with active media relations, recipe development, culinary education, and more. Members of NOA rely on the nonprofit trade association for up-to-date information, government representation, industry-wide networking, as well as consumer outreach. onions-usa.org

SERVES 4 TO 6

2 tablespoons unsalted butter
1 large yellow onion, sliced
4 ounces dry Irish cider
2½ pounds russet potatoes, cut into
    ⅛- to ¼-inch slices
4 cups cold water
½ cup distilled white vinegar
Peanut oil for frying

Finely ground sea salt to taste
4 ounces Cheddar cheese, shredded
4 ounces bacon, cooked and
    crumbled
3 tablespoons sour cream
1 medium jalapeño, seeded and
    chopped
¼ cup chopped red onion

Melt the butter in a medium skillet over medium-high heat. Add the onion to the butter and stir to separate into rings. Cook for 2 minutes, stirring frequently. Reduce the heat to medium-low. Cook for 20 minutes, stirring occasionally. Add the cider. Cook for 15 to 20 minutes or until tender, golden brown and sweet.

Place the potatoes in a large bowl. Add the water and vinegar and stir. Let stand for 15 minutes. Drain the potatoes and pat dry with a kitchen towel.

Fill a 4- to 5-quart pot, deep-frying pan or electric fryer about one-third full with peanut oil. Bring to 375 to 400 degrees. Fry the potatoes in batches for 5 minutes or until golden brown, removing to a paper-towel–lined platter using a slotted spoon. Sprinkle with sea salt.

Layer the potatoes and braised onions on a serving plate. Sprinkle with the Cheddar cheese and bacon. Spoon the sour cream onto the center. Sprinkle with the jalapeño and onion.

Note: *Any type of stock may be used as a substitute for the Irish cider, or the liquid can be omitted. Thin potato slices cook quicker and are crispier. Thicker slices will have crisp edges and more tender centers, like potato wedges or home fries.*

Reggie Rivers' Football Sunday Salmon Salad

SERVES 10

1 (14-ounce) can salmon, sorted
8 ounces cream cheese, softened
1 tablespoon grated onion
1 tablespoon lemon juice
2 teaspoons prepared horseradish

⅓ teaspoon liquid smoke
¼ teaspoon salt
1 cup chopped walnuts or pecans
¼ cup chopped fresh parsley
Balsamic vinegar or tartar sauce

Combine the salmon, cream cheese, onion, lemon juice, horseradish, liquid smoke and salt in a bowl and mix well. Shape to resemble a football on a serving platter. Sprinkle with the walnuts and parsley. Drizzle the balsamic vinegar over the football to resemble football seams and over the platter to resemble field lines. Chill until serving time.

Note: *This delicious salmon football may be placed on salad greens to resemble a gridiron and eaten as a salad (Reggie's favorite), a dip with bread or chips or lettuce wraps.*

For several years, former Denver Broncos player and dynamic speaker Reggie Rivers has served as the master of ceremonies and auctioneer at The Journey, the Junior League of Denver's spring fundraiser. The Journey is an evening of fine dining and inspirational speakers, celebrating the League's impact on the community and the dedicated women who make it so successful.

Shrimp Rémoulade Platter

SERVES 10

1 cup extra-virgin olive oil
¾ cup Creole or coarse-ground
  mustard
¼ cup red wine vinegar
½ cup sliced green onions
¼ cup minced celery

¼ cup minced Italian parsley
1 tablespoon minced garlic
1 tablespoon paprika
Salt to taste
Hot sauce to taste
1 small package shredded lettuce

2 pounds large shrimp with tails
  intact, peeled and deveined,
  cooked
1 pint grape tomatoes
2 cups spicy pickled green beans,
  olives or other pickled vegetables

Whisk the olive oil, Creole mustard and vinegar in a glass bowl. Stir in the green onions, celery, parsley, garlic, paprika, salt and hot sauce. Chill the rémoulade sauce, covered, for 8 to 12 hours.

Spread the lettuce on a platter. Arrange a layer of the shrimp around the edge of the lettuce. Spoon a portion of the rémoulade sauce over the shrimp. Layer with the remaining shrimp and rémoulade sauce. Arrange the grape tomatoes on the platter. Spoon the pickled green beans onto the center of the lettuce. Serve immediately.

Sweet and Spicy Meatballs

MAKES 80

½ cup butter
1½ cups packed light brown sugar
2 teaspoons garlic powder
2 cups ketchup
⅔ cup lemon juice

⅓ cup prepared mustard
⅓ cup Worcestershire sauce
⅓ cup chili sauce
2 teaspoons celery seeds
3 pounds ground chuck

1 cup plain bread crumbs
¾ cup milk
2 eggs, lightly beaten
1½ teaspoons salt
½ teaspoon pepper

Melt the butter in a saucepan. Add the brown sugar and garlic powder. Cook until the brown sugar is melted, stirring constantly. Stir in the ketchup, lemon juice, mustard, Worcestershire sauce, chili sauce and celery seeds. Simmer the sauce, covered, for 40 minutes.

Preheat the oven to 350 degrees.

Combine the ground chuck, bread crumbs, milk, eggs, salt and pepper in a bowl and mix well. Shape into 1-inch meatballs. Arrange the meatballs in a shallow baking dish. Bake for 30 minutes or until cooked through.

Combine the meatballs and sauce in a slow cooker. Cook on Low until serving time.

Note: *If making ahead of time, let the meatballs and sauce cool completely. Combine the meatballs and sauce in an airtight container or covered casserole dish and keep chilled. Cook, covered, in a slow cooker on Low for a few hours or until heated through.*

DISCOVER DENVER

Larimer Square is the best-preserved block of 19th century buildings in downtown Denver. Once lined with the city's finest shopping and dining, by the 1950s Larimer Street was occupied mainly by bars, flophouses, and pawnshops. The city considered the demolition of much of Larimer Street, including the 1400 block now known as Larimer Square. In 1963, former Junior League of Denver member and urban preservationist Dana Crawford founded Larimer Associates, which began buying buildings one at a time and restoring them for new use, thereby saving Larimer Square. The area is now home to a vibrant mix of independent shops, bars, and restaurants.

Cranberry and Pomegranate Bruschetta

SERVES 6 TO 8

1 pound fresh cranberries
1 medium serrano pepper
1 cup sugar
½ cup coarsely chopped fresh basil
¾ cup pomegranate seeds

1 baguette
½ cup extra-virgin olive oil
Sea salt and freshly ground black
    pepper to taste
8 ounces cream cheese, softened

Combine the cranberries, serrano pepper and sugar in a food processor and pulse until the cranberries are coarsely chopped; do not overprocess. Add the basil and pulse a few times or just until coarsely chopped. Spoon the cranberry mixture into a bowl. Stir in the pomegranate seeds. Chill, covered, for 2 hours or longer.

Preheat the oven to 350 degrees. Line a baking sheet with parchment paper.

Cut the baguette diagonally into ¼-inch slices and arrange on the prepared baking sheet. Brush the slices with the olive oil. Sprinkle with salt and pepper. Bake for 14 to 18 minutes or until golden brown, rotating the pan halfway through the baking time. Let stand to cool.

Beat the cream cheese in a bowl until fluffy. Spread each crostini with ½ to 1 tablespoon of the cream cheese, arranging on a plate. Top each with a small spoonful of the Cranberry Relish. Garnish with chopped fresh basil.

Grilled Peaches with Whipped Ricotta Fig Toast

SERVES 16

4 medium peaches, pitted and
   cut into halves
2½ tablespoons honey
½ cup ricotta cheese

3 tablespoons fig spread
16 slices French bread, toasted
⅛ teaspoon sea salt
3 tablespoons chopped fresh mint

Preheat the grill to medium.

Drizzle the peach halves with the honey. Arrange cut sides down on the grill. Grill for 3 to 4 minutes or until grill marks appear. Remove to a cutting board. Cut into slices.

Combine the ricotta cheese and fig spread in a food processor. Process until smooth and creamy. Spread equal portions of the cheese mixture over each toast and top with a peach slice. Sprinkle with the sea salt and mint. Drizzle with additional honey if desired.

Sinful Stuffed Dates

MAKES 12

12 dates, pitted
3 ounces goat cheese
1 tablespoon Sweet Viking Relish™

6 slices bacon, cut lengthwise
   into halves

Preheat the oven to 425 degrees.

Cut the dates lengthwise into halves, cutting to but not through the other side.

Combine the goat cheese and Sweet Viking Relish in a bowl and mix well, adding additional relish if more heat is desired.

Fill the dates with the goat cheese mixture and fold to enclose. Wrap each date with a piece of the bacon and arrange on a rimmed baking sheet. Bake for 10 to 15 minutes or until the bacon is cooked to the desired degree of doneness.

Note: *To make sure the bacon stays wrapped around the dates, place the ends of the bacon face down on the baking sheet.*

Chipotle Shrimp Won Tons

Favorite recipe from Colorado Collage *chosen by Editor Judi Richardson*

MAKES 30

30 won ton wrappers
8 ounces shrimp, cooked, peeled and
   coarsely chopped

1 medium yellow bell pepper, roasted,
   peeled and chopped
1 medium red bell pepper, roasted,
   peeled and chopped

½ cup chopped fresh cilantro
1 chipotle pepper in adobo sauce,
   drained and finely chopped
8 ounces fontina cheese, shredded

Preheat the oven to 350 degrees. Brush 30 mini muffin cups with olive oil.

Press a won ton wrapper in each prepared muffin cup. Bake for 10 minutes or until golden brown. Let stand to cool slightly.

Combine the shrimp, yellow bell pepper, red bell pepper, cilantro, chipotle pepper and fontina cheese in a large bowl and mix well.

Arrange the won ton cups on a baking sheet. Fill the cups with equal portions of the shrimp mixture. Bake for 7 to 10 minutes or until the cheese is melted. Serve warm.

"Colorado Collage, even today, is a wonderful go-to cookbook, offering exceptional recipes that combine fresh and flavorful ingredients requested by today's cuisine. My favorite memory as a chairman is being present to watch the first Colorado Collage come off the press." —Judi Richardson

Game Day Baked Chicken Wings

SERVES 4

1 cup finely grated Parmesan cheese
1 tablespoon dried parsley flakes
1 tablespoon dried oregano
1½ teaspoons smoked paprika

1½ teaspoons salt
2 pounds chicken wings
¾ cup unsalted butter, melted

Preheat the oven to 350 degrees. Line a baking sheet with foil.

Combine the Parmesan cheese, parsley, oregano, paprika and salt in a shallow dish. Dip the chicken wings in the butter and coat with the cheese mixture, arranging on the prepared baking sheet. Bake for 45 minutes.

DISCOVER DENVER

Home of the Colorado Rockies, Coors Field is a Denver gem. During its construction, workers unearthed a dinosaur fossil while excavating an area rumored to be near home plate. The Rockies mascot, a purple triceratops named Dinger, is a nod to the stadium's early history. Although the Rockies added a ball humidor in 2002, Coors Field is still known today as a hitter's park and an exciting place to watch a ball game.

Asian Marinated Chicken Wings

SERVES 12

6 pounds chicken wings
⅔ cup soy sauce
½ cup apple cider vinegar
⅓ cup packed brown sugar
¼ cup sugar

2 teaspoons garlic powder
1 teaspoon ground ginger
3 tablespoons diagonally sliced
  green onions
Sesame seeds to taste

Cut the tips from the chicken wings and cut the wings through the joints into halves.

Combine the soy sauce, vinegar, brown sugar, sugar, garlic powder and ginger in a large sealable plastic bag and mix well. Add the chicken and turn the bag to coat the chicken well. Chill, covered, for 8 to 12 hours, turning over the bag occasionally.

Preheat the oven to 375 degrees.

Remove the chicken from the marinade, arranging in a single layer on 2 baking sheets and reserving the marinade. Bake the wings in the top third of the oven for 45 minutes or until tender and brown, basting twice with the reserved marinade. Remove to a platter. Sprinkle with the green onions and sesame seeds. Garnish with minced multicolored peppers. Serve with Sriracha sauce if desired.

Picnic Skewers

SERVES 12

1 cup balsamic vinegar
¼ cup honey
4 ounces feta cheese, cut into
    12 (½-inch) cubes
12 mint leaves
12 (1-inch) cubes seedless
    watermelon

36 cocktail skewers
4 ounces Brie cheese, cut into
    12 (½-inch) cubes or wedges
12 basil leaves
12 blackberries
12 (1-inch) cubes honeydew melon

6 slices prosciutto, cut lengthwise
    into halves
12 small fresh mozzarella balls
12 (1-inch) cubes cantaloupe

Combine the balsamic vinegar and honey in a small saucepan over high heat. Bring to a boil, stirring frequently. Reduce the heat to low. Cook for 10 to 15 minutes or until the mixture coats the back of a spoon and is reduced to about ½ cup, stirring frequently.

Thread a feta cheese cube, a mint leaf and a watermelon cube on each of 12 cocktail skewers, arranging on a plate. Drizzle with 2 tablespoons of the balsamic reduction.

Thread a wedge of Brie cheese, a folded basil leaf and a blackberry on each of 12 skewers, arranging on a plate. Drizzle with 2 tablespoons of the balsamic reduction.

Thread a honeydew cube, a piece of prosciutto folded accordion style, a mozzarella ball and a cantaloupe cube on each of 12 cocktail skewers, arranging on a plate. Drizzle with 2 tablespoons of the balsamic reduction.

Pancetta and Ricotta-Stuffed Baby Sweet Peppers

MAKES 24

---

2 tablespoons extra-virgin olive oil
3 ounces thinly sliced pancetta,
   chopped
½ medium onion, chopped
¾ cup ricotta cheese

⅓ cup grated Parmigiano-Reggiano
   cheese
½ cup frozen petite peas, thawed
Salt and pepper to taste
24 baby sweet peppers

Preheat the oven to 350 degrees, moving the oven rack to the center position. Spray a baking sheet with nonstick cooking spray.

Heat the olive oil in a medium skillet over medium-high heat. Add the pancetta. Cook for 5 to 7 minutes or until brown and crispy, stirring frequently. Remove to paper towels to drain. Add the onion to the pan drippings. Cook for 5 minutes or until translucent. Let stand to cool for 10 minutes.

Combine the pancetta, onion, ricotta cheese, Parmigiano-Reggiano cheese and peas in a medium bowl and mix well. Season with salt and pepper.

Cut off ½ inch of the stem end of the peppers. Remove the seeds and veins carefully. Fill each pepper with an equal portion of the ricotta mixture, arranging on the prepared baking sheet. Bake for 15 to 18 minutes or until the peppers are tender. Let stand to cool for 10 minutes. Arrange on a platter and serve.

Note: *For a decorative touch, reserve the stem ends of the peppers and replace the stems after arranging the stuffed peppers on the baking sheet.*

Citrus-Marinated Olives

MAKES 1 CUP

1 cup pitted kalamata olives and/or
  green olives
¼ cup fresh orange juice
¼ cup extra-virgin olive oil
2 tablespoons matchstick-cut orange,
  lemon and/or lime peel

2 cloves garlic, very thinly sliced
½ teaspoon red pepper flakes,
  or to taste
Salt to taste

Combine the olives, orange juice, olive oil, citrus peel and garlic in a small bowl and mix well. Season with the red pepper flakes and salt. Chill, covered, for 8 to 12 hours or up to 4 days.

Marinated Mushrooms with Lemon

SERVES 6 TO 8

Juice and grated zest of
  1 medium lemon
4 to 5 tablespoons extra-virgin
  olive oil

Salt and pepper to taste
1 pint button mushrooms
2 tablespoons chopped fresh
  Italian parsley

Combine the lemon juice, lemon zest, olive oil, salt and pepper in a large bowl and mix well.

Wipe the mushrooms with a damp paper towel. Trim any tough stems. Cut the mushrooms into halves (or quarters if large).

Heat a large nonstick skillet over medium heat. Add the mushrooms. Cook for 10 minutes or until most of the liquid from the mushrooms has evaporated, stirring occasionally. Spoon into the lemon juice mixture and mix well. Chill, covered, for 5 hours or up to several days. Stir the mushroom mixture and sprinkle with the parsley just before serving.

Chorizo and Corn Bread–Stuffed Mushrooms

MAKES 24

24 large cremini mushrooms
3 tablespoons extra-virgin olive oil,
 divided
Salt to taste
4 ounces chorizo, casings removed

¼ cup finely chopped celery
¼ cup finely chopped yellow
 bell pepper
1½ cups crumbled corn bread
½ cup shredded Cheddar cheese

½ cup chopped scallions
¼ cup chopped fresh parsley
1 tablespoon chopped pickled
 jalapeño

Preheat the oven to 425 degrees.

Cut the stems from the mushroom caps. Rinse the stems and chop finely. Wipe the caps with a damp paper towel. Combine the caps and 2 tablespoons of the olive oil in a large bowl and toss to coat. Season with salt. Arrange the mushroom caps stem side up on a baking sheet.

Cook the chorizo in the remaining 1 tablespoon olive oil over medium heat for 4 minutes or until cooked through, stirring to crumble. Add the mushroom stems, celery and bell pepper. Cook for 5 minutes or until tender. Let stand to cool.

Add the corn bread, Cheddar cheese, scallions, parsley and jalapeño to the chorizo mixture and mix well. Divide the mixture evenly among the mushroom caps. Bake for 15 to 17 minutes or until the mushrooms are tender and the filling is golden brown. Let stand to cool for 5 minutes. Arrange on a platter. Serve immediately.

Entertaining Tip

Elevate your displays by putting your cake stands, baskets, and boxes to work. Adding height is aesthetically appealing and literally adds new dimension to your table and frees up much-needed space below.

Tapenade Two Ways

SERVES 12

GREEN OLIVE TAPENADE

1 (10-ounce) jar pimento-stuffed
　Spanish Queen olives, drained
2 cloves garlic, minced
2 tablespoons chopped fresh
　Italian parsley

2 tablespoons chopped fresh basil
½ cup walnuts
Juice of ½ medium lemon
¼ cup extra-virgin olive oil

Combine the olives, garlic, parsley, basil, walnuts, lemon juice and olive oil in a food processor and pulse until chopped and well mixed. Serve with warm bread or crackers.

SUN-DRIED TOMATO AND KALAMATA TAPENADE

1 (8-ounce) jar sun-dried tomatoes
½ cup drained kalamata olives
2 tablespoons chopped fresh basil
2 tablespoons chopped fresh
　Italian parsley

2 cloves garlic, minced
Juice of ½ medium lemon
¼ cup extra-virgin olive oil

Drain the sun-dried tomatoes and spread on a paper towel to drain well.

Combine the sun-dried tomatoes, olives, basil, parsley, garlic, lemon juice and olive oil in a food processor and pulse until chopped and well mixed. Serve with warm bread or crackers.

Pesto Cheesecake

SERVES 18 TO 20

1 tablespoon butter, softened
¼ cup fine dry bread crumbs
½ cup plus 2 tablespoons freshly
   grated Parmesan cheese, divided
16 ounces cream cheese, softened
1 cup ricotta cheese

¼ teaspoon salt
⅛ teaspoon cayenne pepper
3 eggs
½ cup pesto
⅓ cup pine nuts

Preheat the oven to 325 degrees. Grease the bottom and side of a 9-inch springform pan with the butter. Coat with a mixture of the bread crumbs and 2 tablespoons of the Parmesan cheese.

Beat the remaining ½ cup Parmesan cheese, cream cheese, ricotta cheese, salt and cayenne pepper in a large mixing bowl until light and fluffy. Beat in the eggs one at a time, mixing well after each addition. Spoon half the mixture into a medium bowl. Stir in the pesto. Spoon into the prepared pan, smoothing the top. Spoon the remaining cream cheese mixture carefully over the pesto mixture, smoothing the top. Sprinkle with the pine nuts or arrange the pine nuts in a spiral pattern over the top.

Bake for 45 to 60 minutes or until the center is set. Remove to a wire rack. Let stand to cool completely. Chill, tightly covered with plastic wrap, for 8 to 12 hours. Run a small sharp knife around the outside of the cheesecake and remove the side of the pan. Place the cheesecake on a platter. Garnish the top with fresh basil leaves. Serve with crackers.

Shrimp Louis Dip

SERVES 6 TO 8

2 cups finely chopped cooked shrimp
1 cup sour cream
1 cup mayonnaise
⅓ cup finely chopped green
  bell pepper

¼ cup chili sauce
1 tablespoon prepared horseradish
¼ teaspoon salt
¼ teaspoon pepper

Combine the shrimp, sour cream, mayonnaise, bell pepper, chili sauce, horseradish, salt and pepper in a bowl and mix well. Chill, covered, for 2 hours or longer. Spoon into a serving dish. Serve with crackers or baguette slices.

Reuben Dip

SERVES 8 TO 10

8 ounces thinly sliced corned beef,
  chopped
1 cup drained and chopped
  sauerkraut
1¼ cups sour cream

8 ounces cream cheese, softened
¼ cup shredded Swiss cheese
3 tablespoons ketchup
2 tablespoons mustard
½ teaspoon garlic powder

Preheat the oven to 350 degrees. Spray an 8×8-inch glass baking dish with nonstick cooking spray.

Combine the corned beef, sauerkraut, sour cream, cream cheese, Swiss cheese, ketchup, mustard and garlic powder in a large bowl and mix well. Spread evenly in the prepared baking dish.

Cover with foil. Bake for 30 minutes or until heated through and the edges are bubbly. Serve with toasted mini rye bread slices or rye crackers.

Game Day Dip

SERVES 10

6 chicken breasts
12 ounces buffalo wing sauce

16 ounces cream cheese, chopped
16 ounces blue cheese salad dressing

Combine the chicken with enough water to cover in a large saucepan. Bring to a boil. Boil for 15 to 20 minutes or until cooked through; drain.

Preheat the oven to 325 degrees.

Shred the chicken and spread in a 9×13-inch baking dish. Pour the buffalo wing sauce over the chicken and toss to coat.

Combine the cream cheese and salad dressing in a saucepan. Cook over medium heat until the cream cheese is melted and the mixture is smooth, stirring frequently. Pour over the chicken mixture and stir to mix. Bake for 20 minutes. Serve with blue corn tortilla chips and celery sticks.

Creamy Goat Cheese and Jalapeño Dip

SERVES 6

2 tablespoons unsalted butter
1½ cups chopped yellow onion
2 cups fresh sweet corn kernels
1 teaspoon salt
½ teaspoon cayenne pepper
1 tablespoon chopped garlic

1 medium jalapeño, seeded and
   chopped
16 ounces goat cheese, crumbled
½ cup heavy cream
Chopped fresh cilantro to taste

Melt the butter in a medium saucepan over medium heat. Cook the onion, corn, salt and cayenne pepper in the butter for 6 minutes, stirring frequently. Stir in the garlic and jalapeño. Cook for 2 minutes, stirring frequently. Add the goat cheese and cream. Cook until the cheese is melted, stirring frequently. Spoon into a serving dish. Sprinkle with cilantro and serve immediately, keeping dish warm.

Hot Pepper Peach Dip

SERVES 10

16 ounces cream cheese, softened
½ cup peach preserves
2 medium jalapeños, seeded and
 chopped

3 tablespoons chopped green onions
2 cups shredded Pepper Jack cheese

Preheat the oven to 400 degrees.

Beat the cream cheese and peach preserves in a mixing bowl until blended. Stir in the jalapeños, green onions and Pepper Jack cheese. Spoon into an 8×8-inch baking dish. Bake for 15 minutes or until hot and bubbly. Serve immediately with crackers, chips or celery.

Cannoli Fruit Dip

SERVES 8

15 ounces whole-milk ricotta cheese
8 ounces mascarpone cheese
¼ cup honey
Grated zest of ½ medium orange

½ teaspoon vanilla extract
¼ teaspoon ground cinnamon
¼ cup mini semisweet chocolate chips

Beat the ricotta cheese and mascarpone cheese in a mixing bowl until smooth. Mix in the honey, orange zest, vanilla extract and cinnamon. Stir in the chocolate chips. Serve with strawberries, apple slices and cinnamon graham crackers.

Basil Parmesan Cheddar Bites

MAKES 24

2 1/2 cups shredded Cheddar cheese
6 tablespoons butter, softened
5 tablespoons half-and-half
1 teaspoon kosher salt

1 1/2 cups all-purpose flour
1 1/2 cups grated Parmesan cheese
1/4 cup finely chopped fresh basil

Preheat the oven to 350 degrees. Line 2 baking sheets with parchment paper.

Beat the Cheddar cheese, butter, half-and-half and salt at medium speed in a mixing bowl until blended. Add the flour, Parmesan cheese and basil gradually, beating constantly. Beat just until mixed.

Divide the dough into 3 equal portions on a well-floured work surface. Roll into a 1/4-inch-thick circle. Cut with 2- to 3-inch cookie cutters of desired shape. Arrange 1 inch apart on the prepared baking sheets. Bake for 11 to 14 minutes or until golden brown. Remove to wire racks. Let stand to cool for 30 minutes.

Note: *These crackers are cut out using cookie cutters, so they can be customized for just about any type of party or gathering.*

Entertaining Tip

Menu seasonality matters. Not only can it save money, but it also shapes your guests' experience. Serving rich and stick-to-your-bones dishes in the middle of summer will leave your guests feeling heavy and uncomfortable. Save those meals for winter and opt for lighter fare that can be served chilled or grilled outside.

Lavash Crackers 5 Ways to Sunday

SERVES 6

1 large pinch saffron threads,
  crumbled
1¼ cups hot water
1 envelope active dry yeast
1 teaspoon sugar

4 cups bread flour
¼ cup plus 1 tablespoon
  extra-virgin olive oil, divided
1 tablespoon sesame seed oil
2 tablespoons honey

2 teaspoons sea salt
Lavash Topping Options (below)
Flaky sea salt to taste
  (such as Maldon)

Crumble the saffron over the water in a small bowl. Let stand to steep until the water temperature is 100 to 110 degrees. Stir in the yeast and sugar. Let stand for 5 minutes or until foamy.

Combine the flour, ¼ cup of the olive oil, sesame seed oil, honey, 2 teaspoons salt and yeast mixture in a mixing bowl. Mix with the dough hook at medium-low speed for 5 to 10 minutes or until supple and firm. Divide the dough into 5 equal portions. Shape each portion into a ball.

Coat a large bowl with the remaining 1 tablespoon olive oil. Add the dough balls, turning to coat all sides. Cover with a damp towel. Let rest for 15 minutes.

Preheat the oven to 325 degrees, moving the oven rack to the top position.

Roll each ball into a thin 12 × 16-inch rectangle on a lightly floured work surface. Brush the surface of each rectangle with water. Sprinkle with generous portions of one of the Lavash Topping Options. Finish with flaky sea salt, pressing the seasonings in lightly using a rolling pin. Remove to baking sheets. Bake for 30 to 40 minutes or until puffed and lightly browned. Transfer to wire racks to cool. Break into large pieces to serve.

LAVASH TOPPING OPTIONS

Herbes de Provence to taste
Everything bagel seasoning to taste
Mixture of ¼ cup grated Parmesan cheese and grated zest of 1 large lemon
Mixture of poppy seeds and white and black sesame seeds to taste
Za'atar to taste

Note: *The dough may be flattened using a pasta machine. The dough is versatile and may be baked in one sheet or cut into the desired lengths and shapes.*

Chili Lime Popcorn

SERVES 6

---

2 tablespoons coconut oil
Juice of 1 medium lime

1½ teaspoons chili powder
10 cups premium popped corn

Grated zest of 2 medium limes
Salt to taste

Melt the coconut oil in a small saucepan over medium heat. Remove from the heat. Stir in the lime juice and chili powder.

Place the popcorn in an extra-large bowl. Drizzle with the lime juice mixture. Sprinkle with the lime zest and salt and stir to coat well.

JaMocha Caramel Popcorn

SERVES 7

14 cups premium popped corn
4 ounces chopped pecans
1 cup unsalted butter

½ cup light corn syrup
1½ tablespoons baking cocoa
1 tablespoon instant espresso

1½ teaspoons ground cinnamon
1 teaspoon salt
2 cups firmly packed brown sugar

Preheat the oven to 200 degrees. Line a large baking sheet with a silicone mat or parchment paper.

Combine the popcorn and pecans in an extra-large bowl and toss to mix.

Combine the butter, corn syrup, cocoa, espresso, cinnamon and salt in a large saucepan with high sides. Cook over medium heat until the butter is melted, stirring constantly. Stir in the brown sugar. Cook until the brown sugar is dissolved and the mixture is smooth, stirring constantly. Simmer for 5 minutes or until the mixture reaches the hard ball stage (250 degrees at sea level; subtract 1 degree for every 500 feet of altitude) without stirring; large bubbles should form over the entire surface.

Pour the brown sugar mixture carefully over the popcorn mixture and fold in using a rubber spatula; do not overmix. Spread on the prepared baking sheet. Bake for 1 hour, stirring every 20 minutes for even baking. Let stand to cool completely. Store in an airtight container.

Slow-Burn Caramel Popcorn

SERVES 6

½ cup butter
1 cup firmly packed brown sugar
¼ cup light corn syrup

1 tablespoon molasses
¾ teaspoon Louisiana hot sauce
¾ teaspoon cayenne pepper

¼ teaspoon salt
20 drops red food coloring (optional)
10 cups premium popped corn

Preheat the oven to 200 degrees. Line a baking sheet with a silicone mat or parchment paper.

Melt the butter in a medium saucepan with high sides over medium heat. Stir in the brown sugar, corn syrup, molasses, hot sauce, cayenne pepper and salt using a wooden spoon. Cook until smooth, stirring constantly. Simmer for 5 minutes or until the mixture reaches the hard ball stage (250 degrees at sea level; subtract 1 degree for every 500 feet of altitude) without stirring; large bubbles should form over the entire surface. Remove from the heat. Stir in the food coloring; mixture may spatter.

Place the popcorn in an extra-large bowl. Pour the brown sugar mixture carefully over the popcorn and fold in using a rubber spatula; do not overmix. Spread on the prepared baking sheet. Bake for 1 hour or to hard-crack stage, stirring every 15 minutes. Let stand to cool completely. Break into chunks. Store, covered, in a dry place.

Orange Rosemary Gin Rickey

SERVES 4

6 ounces gin
4 ounces Orange Rosemary Simple Syrup
  (recipe below)
12 ounces club soda

Fill a cocktail shaker with ice. Add the gin and Orange Rosemary Simple Syrup. Strain into 4 martini or low ball glasses. Divide the club soda evenly among the glasses. Add ice if serving in low ball glasses. Garnish each beverage with a sprig of rosemary and strips of orange peel.

ORANGE ROSEMARY SIMPLE SYRUP

1 medium orange
¼ cup loosely packed fresh rosemary
  leaves

2 tablespoons honey
½ cup boiling water

Peel the orange using a vegetable peeler. Combine the orange peel, rosemary and honey in a heatproof jar or bowl. Add the boiling water. Let steep for 20 minutes, stirring occasionally; strain. Let stand to cool completely. May store, covered, in the refrigerator for up to 1 week.

Pumpkin Spice Martini

SERVES 2

4 ounces vanilla cinnamon Irish cream
  liqueur
2 ounces pumpkin spice vodka

2 ounces vanilla vodka
Ground cinnamon to taste

Place a handful of ice in a martini shaker. Add the liqueur, pumpkin spice vodka and vanilla vodka and shake. Strain into 2 martini glasses. Sprinkle with cinnamon.

Ashes of Roses: A Proper Gimlet

Archetype Distillery, based in Denver, is built around a passion for creating quality spirits and fostering a sense of community. With Archangel Vodka and Archrival Gin, they are dedicated to raising Denver's spirits, one drink at a time. archetypedistillery.com

SERVES 1

1½ ounces Archrival Gin™
2 ounces fresh lime juice
1 teaspoon simple syrup,
   or to taste
Tincture of activated charcoal
   to taste

Fill a cocktail shaker with ice. Add the gin, lime juice and simple syrup and stir or shake. Strain into a glass. Stir in activated charcoal. Garnish with a cucumber slice or lime peel. Serve immediately.

Bada Bing Cocktail

SERVES 2

1½ ounces peach schnapps, chilled
1½ ounces lime vodka, chilled
1 ounce lime juice
1 ounce simple syrup

Fill a cocktail shaker with ice. Add the schnapps, vodka, lime juice and simple syrup and shake. Strain into a martini glass. Garnish with a lime wedge.

Note: *Simple syrup is sold in liquor stores but can be made at home. Cook equal amounts of sugar and water in a saucepan over medium heat until the sugar is dissolved, stirring constantly. Let stand to cool completely.*

Blood Orange Cocktail

SERVES 2

3 ounces tequila
1 ounce fresh lime juice

1 ounce Triple Sec
3 ounces blood orange soda

Fill a cocktail shaker with ice. Add the tequila, lime juice and Triple Sec and shake. Fill 2 glasses with ice. Strain into the prepared glasses. Top off with equal portions of the soda. Garnish with orange slices and mint leaves.

Note: *Depending on what soda you use, this drink can be anywhere from a bright sunny orange to a deep reddish pink. Either way, it's a refreshing and beautiful cocktail.*

WATERMELON ROSÉ MARGARITAS

Watermelon Rosé Margaritas

SERVES 12

12 ounces Rosé Simple Syrup (recipe below)
8 ounces lime juice
8 ounces watermelon juice or purée

8 ounces rosé wine
8 ounces Triple Sec
12 ounces tequila
2 medium limes, cut into slices

Combine the Rosé Simple Syrup, lime juice, watermelon juice, rosé, Triple Sec and tequila in a large pitcher and stir. Fill 12 glasses with ice. Divide the margaritas evenly among the prepared glasses. Squeeze a lime slice over each margarita, dropping the lime into the glass. Serve immediately.

ROSÉ SIMPLE SYRUP

1 cup rosé wine
1 cup sugar

Combine the rosé and sugar in a small saucepan over medium heat. Cook until the sugar is dissolved, whisking constantly. Remove from the heat. Let stand to cool completely.

Cranberry Grapefruit Sparkler

SERVES 1

1 ounce cranberry juice
1 ounce grapefruit juice
½ ounce elderflower liqueur
2 to 3 ounces Prosecco or Champagne

Combine the cranberry juice, grapefruit juice and liqueur in a glass. Add the desired amount of ice. Top off with the Prosecco. Garnish with 2 or 3 fresh raspberries. Serve immediately.

Note: *For 10 servings, combine 2 cups cranberry juice, 2 cups grapefruit juice and 1½ cups elderflower liqueur in a 2½-quart pitcher and stir. Add 1 bottle Prosecco or Champagne. Fill 10 glasses with ice and add the juice mixture. Garnish beverages with equal portions of 6 ounces of fresh raspberries.*

Fire and Iced Tea

SERVES 10

1 cup powdered unsweetened
  instant iced tea mix
1 cup powdered orange-flavored
  drink mix (such as Tang)

2 gallons water
1 quart cinnamon whiskey

Combine the iced tea mix, drink mix, water and whiskey in a large pitcher and stir until the mixes are dissolved. Chill until serving time. Fill 10 glasses with ice. Divide the tea evenly among the glasses. Garnish each beverage with a sprig of mint and an orange slice.

Ginger Fizzy Drink

Recipe from The Teaching Kitchen at the Children's Museum of Denver at Marsico Campus

SERVES 4

1 (1- to 2-inch) piece ginger root
3 tablespoons water
2 tablespoons agave nectar
2 cups carbonated water
16 ice cubes

Peel the ginger using a metal spoon. Combine the ginger, water and agave nectar in a blender. Process for 15 to 20 seconds or until smooth; strain.

Fill each of 4 glasses with ½ cup carbonated water. Add 1 teaspoon of the ginger mixture to each glass and stir until the bubbles subside. Add 4 ice cubes to each drink. Garnish each with a slice of lemon or lime. Taste and add additional ginger mixture if needed. Enjoy!

Mayan Mocha

SERVES 4

2 ounces dark chocolate, chopped
2 cups milk
1 cup hot strong coffee
½ teaspoon vanilla extract
½ teaspoon ground cinnamon
¼ teaspoon ground cayenne pepper
½ cup coffee liqueur (optional)

Combine the dark chocolate and milk in a heavy saucepan. Cook over medium heat until the chocolate is melted, whisking constantly. Add the coffee, vanilla extract, cinnamon, cayenne pepper and coffee liqueur. Cook until heated through, stirring frequently; do not boil. Serve hot. May serve with marshmallows (recipe page 287).

Breakfast & Breads

spring
brunch

HOMEMADE YOGURT PARFAIT BAR
WITH MAPLE ORANGE GRANOLA

HAM AND CHEESE QUICHE

SPRING SALAD WITH ASPARAGUS

CUCUMBER TEA SANDWICHES

CLASSIC CHICKEN SALAD
SANDWICHES

HUMMINGBIRD CAKE
WITH
CREAM CHEESE
FROSTING

Menu

Spring Awakenings

SPRING

Homemade Yogurt Parfaits ~ 70

Ham and Cheese Quiche ~ 64

Spring Salad with Asparagus ~ 88

Classic Chicken Salad Sandwiches ~ 236

Cucumber Tea Sandwiches ~ 236

Hummingbird Cake with Cream Cheese Icing ~ 256

A Peach of a Cookie ~ 281

A Breakfast with Purpose

Every year, the Junior League of Denver hosts its annual Legislative Breakfast at the State Capitol. Legislators from all over Colorado join JLD's Public Policy Council, Board of Directors, and members to discuss legislation important to the League and its focus. JLD has a proud history of public policy and advocacy. In 1987, JLD was the first League in the United States to hire a government affairs specialist to monitor, advocate, and support important pieces of legislation at the State Capitol. Most recently, the League has supported legislation affecting children's education and health, women's self-sufficiency, and affordable childcare.

Fresh Corn Quiche

SERVES 6

1⅓ cups half-and-half
3 eggs
1 small onion, chopped
1 tablespoon sugar
1 tablespoon all-purpose flour

1 teaspoon salt
3 tablespoons butter, melted
2 cups fresh corn or thawed
    frozen corn
1 (9-inch) unbaked pie shell

Cook the half-and-half in a saucepan or double boiler over medium-low heat until steamy and the edge is slightly bubbly, stirring frequently; do not boil. Let stand to cool.

Preheat the oven to 375 degrees.

Combine the eggs, onion, sugar, flour and salt in a food processor. Add the butter and half-and-half. Process until blended. Fold in the corn.

Pour the egg mixture into the pie shell. Bake for 45 minutes or until puffed and lightly browned. Cut into wedges and serve.

Quiche Lorraine

SERVES 6

1 refrigerated pie pastry
1½ cups shredded Swiss cheese
2 tablespoons all-purpose flour
4 eggs
1½ cups half-and-half
½ teaspoon salt

¼ teaspoon ground black pepper
¼ teaspoon sugar
⅔ cup chopped bacon
⅓ cup grated or finely chopped
    sweet onion

Preheat the oven to 350 degrees. Unfold the pastry. Fit into a pie plate and trim the edge.

Combine the Swiss cheese and flour in a bowl and toss to mix.

Beat the eggs, half-and-half, salt, pepper and sugar in a bowl. Spread the bacon, onion and Swiss cheese mixture in the pie shell. Pour the egg mixture evenly over the bacon mixture. Bake for 40 to 45 minutes or until a wooden pick inserted near the center comes out clean.

Baked Eggs in Greens

SERVES 12

½ cup water
2 pounds fresh spinach
2 tablespoons extra-virgin olive oil
1 medium onion, chopped
4 cloves garlic, minced
1 pound button mushrooms,
   thinly sliced

¾ cup cream or half-and-half
½ teaspoon kosher salt
Black pepper to taste
Ground nutmeg to taste
12 eggs
Finely grated Parmesan cheese
   to taste (optional)

Preheat the oven to 450 degrees.

Bring the water to a boil in a large saucepan or skillet. Add the spinach. Cook until wilted, stirring frequently and cooking in batches if necessary; drain in a colander. Rinse with cool water and drain. Squeeze out any excess liquid. Chop the spinach coarsely.

Heat the olive oil in a large skillet over medium heat. Sauté the onion in the hot oil for 10 minutes or just until golden brown. Add the garlic. Sauté for 2 minutes. Add the mushrooms. Cook for 6 to 8 minutes or until tender and most of the liquid has evaporated, stirring frequently. Stir in the cream, salt, pepper, nutmeg and spinach. Bring to a simmer. Simmer for 3 minutes. Remove from the heat.

Spoon the mixture into a 9×13-inch or larger baking dish. May chill, covered, for 8 to 12 hours if making ahead. Make 12 wells in the mixture using a tablespoon. Break an egg into each well.

Bake for 15 to 30 minutes or until the eggs are done to taste, rotating the baking dish after 8 to 10 minutes; the center eggs may not set completely. Sprinkle with Parmesan cheese and serve immediately.

Note: *Two cups of frozen spinach may be used instead of fresh spinach. Thaw the spinach and drain well, squeezing out any excess liquid.*

DISCOVER DENVER

The Denver Botanic Gardens celebrates beautiful plants and collections from all over the world. At its two locations, York Street and Chatfield Farms, the Gardens hosts wonderful events throughout the year to bring families and the community together. The Gardens offers many learning opportunities as well as fascinating, year-round art and exhibits. Annual events include their Summer Concert Series, fall festivals, plant shows, and winter festivities like the popular Blossoms of Light™.

Bacon, Leek and Cheese Mini Quiches

MAKES 4 DOZEN

8 slices bacon, chopped
3 cups thinly sliced leeks including
    light green tops, rinsed and drained
2 eggs
2 egg yolks
1¼ cups half-and-half
1 cup grated cheese, such as
    Cheddar, Gruyère or
    Jalapeño Cheddar

2 teaspoons dried thyme
1 teaspoon kosher salt
½ teaspoon pepper
¼ teaspoon ground nutmeg
2 (17-ounce) packages frozen puff
    pastry, thawed

Cook the bacon in a medium skillet over medium-high heat for 8 to 10 minutes or until brown and crisp, stirring frequently. Remove to paper towels using a slotted spoon, reserving 1 to 2 tablespoons drippings in the skillet. Cook the leeks in the reserved drippings over medium heat for 5 to 7 minutes or until tender, stirring occasionally. Let stand to cool.

Beat the eggs and egg yolks in a medium bowl. Add the half-and-half, cheese, thyme, salt, pepper and nutmeg and mix well. Stir in the bacon and leeks.

Preheat the oven to 400 degrees, moving the oven racks to the top third and bottom third positions. Spray 48 miniature muffin cups with nonstick cooking spray.

Roll each puff pastry sheet into a 10×18-inch rectangle on a lightly floured surface using a floured rolling pin. Cut into a total of 48 circles using a 3-inch biscuit cutter. Fit each circle evenly into a prepared muffin cup, pressing up the sides. Fill each cup with about 1 tablespoonful of the egg mixture, filling the cups completely. Bake for 20 minutes or until the crust is golden brown, rearranging the pans halfway through the baking time. Garnish with a sprig of fresh thyme.

Entertaining Tip

Mismatched china adds a fun detail to any table or buffet. Buy interesting plates or serving dishes individually at thrift or antique stores. Stick with a similar color scheme or theme and amass a collection that works beautifully together as a unique whole.

Ham and Cheese Quiche

SERVES 6

5 eggs	12 ounces ham steak, chopped
1½ cups milk	⅓ cup loosely packed
Salt and pepper to taste	chopped chives
2 cups grated Colby-Jack cheese	1 (9-inch) unbaked deep-dish
2 tablespoons all-purpose flour	pie shell

Preheat the oven to 350 degrees.

Whisk the eggs in a large bowl. Whisk in the milk, salt and pepper. Combine the Colby-Jack cheese and flour in a small bowl and toss to coat.

Add the cheese, ham and chives to the egg mixture and mix well. Spoon evenly into the pie shell. Bake for 45 to 55 minutes or until set and light brown, covering the edge with foil or a piecrust shield if needed to prevent overbrowning. Let stand for 15 minutes before serving.

Note: *As an alternative, omit the chives, substitute Swiss cheese for the Colby-Jack cheese and add 1 cup chopped cooked spinach. May use refrigerated pie pastry fit into a 9-inch pie pan or tart pan with 2-inch sides.*

Brunch Eggs

SERVES 12

12 slices Canadian bacon	½ teaspoon black pepper
12 ounces shredded Swiss cheese	⅓ cup grated Parmesan cheese
12 eggs	1 teaspoon paprika
1 cup whipping cream	¼ cup chopped fresh Italian parsley
½ teaspoon salt	

Preheat the oven to 425 degrees. Grease a 9×13-inch baking dish lightly.

Arrange the Canadian bacon in a single layer in the prepared baking dish. Sprinkle with the Swiss cheese. May chill, covered, for 8 to 12 hours if making ahead.

Break an egg over each slice of Canadian bacon. Pour the whipping cream evenly over the eggs. Sprinkle with the salt and pepper. Bake for 10 minutes. Sprinkle with the Parmesan cheese and paprika. Bake for 8 to 10 minutes or until set. Sprinkle with the parsley. Let stand for 10 minutes. Cut into 12 pieces and serve over English muffins or bagels.

HAM AND CHEESE QUICHE

Vegan Tofu Scramble

SERVES 4 TO 6

1 (14- to 16-ounce) package
   extra-firm tofu
1 cup raw cashews
1 tablespoon extra-virgin olive oil
1 cup chopped onion
Sea salt to taste
1 cup chopped mushrooms

1 cup coarsely chopped zucchini
1 tablespoon tahini
1 tablespoon yellow or white
   miso paste
2 to 3 tablespoons nutritional yeast,
   or to taste
1 teaspoon ground turmeric

¼ cup water
¼ cup loosely packed fresh cilantro
3 cups finely chopped fresh spinach
Black pepper to taste
½ medium avocado, sliced

Place the tofu between layers of paper towels or clean kitchen towels. Place a heavy flat-bottom plate or bowl on top. Let stand for 15 minutes or up to a few hours. Crumble the tofu coarsely.

Soak the cashews in enough water to cover in a bowl for 30 minutes or up to 2 hours.

Heat the olive oil in a large skillet or sauté pan over medium-high heat. Sauté the onion in the hot oil for 2 minutes, seasoning generously with salt. Add the mushrooms. Sauté for 3 minutes. Add the zucchini. Sauté for 3 minutes. Cook for 5 minutes or until the onion is translucent and the zucchini is tender and cooked through, stirring frequently.

Process the tahini, miso paste, yeast, turmeric, cashews, ¼ cup water and cilantro in a blender or food processor or in a bowl using an immersion blender until blended.

Add the tofu, spinach and tahini mixture to the zucchini mixture and mix well. Cook until the spinach is fully cooked, stirring occasionally; do not overcook. Season with salt and pepper. Spoon into a serving dish. Top with the avocado and serve.

Eggs in Tomato Sauce with Sausage

SERVES 6 TO 8

---

1 pound Italian sweet pork sausage,
  casings removed
1 large onion, finely chopped
5 cloves garlic, minced
2 medium red bell peppers, finely
  chopped
1 tablespoon chopped fresh oregano
1½ teaspoons ground cumin

1½ teaspoons ground coriander
1 teaspoon ground turmeric
1 teaspoon curry powder
¼ teaspoon cayenne pepper
¼ teaspoon white pepper
2 teaspoons smoked paprika
1 teaspoon salt

1 (28-ounce) can petite diced
  tomatoes
1¼ cups canned coconut milk
6 to 8 medium eggs
6 ounces crumbled feta cheese
¼ cup coarsely chopped fresh
  Italian parsley

Preheat the oven to 350 degrees, moving the oven rack to the top position.

Cook the sausage in a large ovenproof sauté pan or paella pan over medium-low heat just until no longer pink, stirring to crumble; do not brown. Remove to a colander or paper towels to drain, reserving the pan drippings.

Sauté the onion and garlic in the reserved drippings over medium-low heat until translucent; do not brown. Add the bell peppers, oregano, cumin, coriander, turmeric, curry powder, cayenne pepper, white pepper, paprika and salt. Sauté for 2 to 3 minutes. Stir in the undrained tomatoes, coconut milk and sausage. Simmer over medium heat for 15 minutes or until thickened. Reduce the heat to low.

Make 6 to 8 wells in the mixture using a spoon. Break an egg into each well. Sprinkle with the feta cheese. Bake for 15 minutes or until the eggs are firm but not dry. Sprinkle with the parsley and serve immediately.

Chili Cheddar Frittata

SERVES 6

---

1 (4-ounce) can mild green chiles or
  jalapeños, or 3 roasted fresh green
  chiles, chopped
8 ounces sharp white Cheddar
  cheese, shredded

⅓ cup oil-packed sun-dried tomatoes,
  drained and chopped
½ to 1 cup chopped fresh basil
9 eggs

Preheat the oven to 350 degrees. Spray a 10-inch round or 9×9-inch baking dish with nonstick cooking spray.

Drain the green chiles, reserving the liquid. Layer the Cheddar cheese, green chiles, sun-dried tomatoes and basil in the prepared baking dish. Beat the eggs and reserved green chile liquid in a large bowl. Pour over the layers in the baking dish. Bake for 30 minutes or until set.

Decadent French Toast Soufflé

SERVES 8

8 ounces croissants (about
   4 croissants)
8 ounces cream cheese, softened
½ cup butter, softened

1¼ cups good-quality
   maple syrup, divided
10 eggs
3 cups half-and-half

1 teaspoon ground cinnamon
Ground nutmeg to taste
2 tablespoons chopped pecans
Powdered sugar to taste

Break the croissants into ½-inch pieces. Process in a food processor just until coarsely chopped. Spread in a buttered 9 × 13-inch baking dish.

Beat the cream cheese, butter and ¼ cup of the maple syrup in a mixing bowl until fluffy. Drop by spoonfuls onto the croissants.

Beat the eggs, half-and-half, ½ cup of the maple syrup, cinnamon and nutmeg in a bowl until well mixed. Pour evenly over the croissants. Chill, covered, for 8 to 24 hours.

Preheat the oven to 350 degrees.

Bake the French toast, uncovered, for 70 minutes or until well browned and the center is almost set. Sprinkle with the pecans and powdered sugar. Garnish with berries. Warm the remaining maple syrup and serve with the French toast.

Ginger Cream Sauce for Fresh Fruit

SERVES 6

1 cup heavy cream
3 tablespoons minced peeled
   fresh ginger root

¼ teaspoon grated lemon zest
3 egg yolks
3 tablespoons sugar

Combine the cream, ginger and lemon zest in a small saucepan. Bring to a boil. Remove from the heat. Let stand, covered, for 20 minutes.

Beat the egg yolks and sugar in a mixing bowl until pale yellow. Whisk the egg mixture into the cream mixture. Cook over low heat to 160 degrees on a candy thermometer. Strain through a mesh sieve. Chill the sauce, covered, until serving time. Serve over fruit or a favorite dessert.

Homemade Yogurt Parfaits with Maple Orange Granola and Fruit Sauces

SERVES 6

---

32 ounces whole milk
1 package yogurt starter, or
   3 tablespoons plain yogurt

Maple Orange Granola (recipe below)
Fruit Sauces (recipe page 71)
6 peeled orange slices

Pour the milk into a sanitized 2-quart saucepan. Cook over medium heat to 180 degrees on a candy thermometer. Maintain the milk at 180 degrees for 5 minutes, stirring occasionally with a sterilized flat-edge wooden spoon. Remove from the heat. Stir just until the thermometer reads 110 degrees, placing in a bowl of cold water for quicker cooling if desired.

Pour a small amount of the warm milk into a small bowl. Whisk in the yogurt starter. Return to the saucepan and mix well.

Incubate the mixture in a yogurt machine according to the manufacturer's instructions for 4 to 10 hours; the longer the incubation time, the tangier and thicker the yogurt will be. Chill, covered, for up to a few days. May incubate the yogurt in a covered container wrapped securely in clean towels in a cold oven with the oven light on or incubate in a slow cooker using the yogurt setting.

Fill each of 6 parfait cups with alternating layers of Maple Orange Granola, yogurt and Fruit Sauces. Top each with an orange slice.

MAPLE ORANGE GRANOLA

---

3 cups old-fashioned whole oats
1 cup pepitas
1 cup almonds, coarsely chopped
½ cup shredded unsweetened
   coconut

¼ cup dried wild blueberries
   or currants
3 tablespoons chia seeds
3 tablespoons flax seeds
½ teaspoon ground cinnamon
½ teaspoon ground cardamom

¼ teaspoon ground nutmeg
¼ teaspoon salt
½ cup maple agave syrup
½ cup honey
⅓ cup extra-virgin olive oil
Grated zest of 1 large orange

Preheat the oven to 300 degrees. Line a baking sheet with a silicone mat or parchment paper.

Combine the oats, pepitas, almonds, coconut, dried blueberries, chia seeds, flax seeds, cinnamon, cardamom, nutmeg and salt in an extra-large bowl and toss to mix. Combine the syrup, honey, olive oil and orange zest in a bowl and mix well. Add to the oats mixture and stir to coat. Spread loosely on the prepared baking sheet; do not flatten.

Bake for 40 to 60 minutes or until dry, stirring occasionally. Let stand to cool; the mixture will become crispy.

FRUIT SAUCES

12 ounces fresh blackberries
1 tablespoon honey
1 teaspoon vanilla extract
1 tablespoon powdered sugar (optional)
1 (20-ounce) can pineapple chunks
1 teaspoon ground ginger

For blackberry sauce, purée the blackberries with the honey and vanilla extract until pulpy and liquefied, adding the powdered sugar if the mixture is too tart. Strain through a fine mesh sieve if desired.

For ginger pineapple sauce, drain the pineapple, reserving the juice. Combine ¼ cup of the reserved juice, pineapple and ginger in a bowl. Process using an immersion blender until pulpy, adding additional juice if needed; sauce should be thick and pulpy but not runny.

Grapefruit with Wine Syrup

SERVES 6 TO 8

7 large red grapefruit
½ cup dry red wine, such as zinfandel
½ cup sugar

Peel 6 of the grapefruit over a bowl using a sharp serrated knife, removing the white pith. Cut between the membranes to remove the segments, placing the segments in the bowl. Chill, covered, for 30 minutes or up to 24 hours.

Juice the remaining grapefruit. Combine the juice, wine and sugar in a small saucepan. Bring to a boil. Boil until reduced by half. Let the syrup stand to cool. May chill, covered, for up to 24 hours.

Divide the grapefruit evenly among 6 to 8 small bowls. Top with equal portions of the syrup.

Cherry Cornmeal Scones

MAKES 10 TO 12

2 cups all-purpose flour
1 tablespoon baking powder
¾ teaspoon baking soda
1½ cups medium-grind yellow
 cornmeal
1 cup sugar, divided

¼ teaspoon kosher salt
1 cup cold unsalted butter, cut into
 1-inch slices
1 cup dried sweet cherries
1¼ cups buttermilk

Preheat the oven to 425 degrees, moving the oven rack to the middle position. Line a baking sheet with parchment paper.

Sift the flour, baking powder and baking soda into a large mixing bowl. Add the cornmeal, ¾ cup of the sugar and salt and stir to mix. Beat in the butter at low speed for 4 minutes or until the mixture resembles small peas. Stir in the dried cherries.

Make a well in the center of the flour mixture. Pour the buttermilk into the well and stir just until blended. Let stand for 5 minutes.

Shape the dough gently into 2-inch balls, arranging 2 inches apart on the prepared baking sheet. Sprinkle evenly with the remaining ¼ cup sugar. Place the baking sheet in the oven. Reduce the oven temperature to 375 degrees. Bake for 20 to 25 minutes or until the scones are golden brown. Remove to a wire rack to cool.

Pumpkin Apple Bread

SERVES 24

1 (16-ounce) can pumpkin purée
¾ cup vegetable oil
2¼ cups sugar
4 large eggs

3 cups all-purpose flour
2 teaspoons baking soda
¾ teaspoon salt
1½ teaspoons ground cinnamon

1 teaspoon ground nutmeg
2 medium apples, peeled and grated
Cinnamon-Sugar Topping
    (recipe below)

Preheat the oven to 350 degrees. Grease two 5×9-inch loaf pans

Combine the pumpkin, vegetable oil, sugar and eggs in a bowl and mix well. Add the flour, baking soda, salt, cinnamon and nutmeg and mix well. Fold in the apples. Spoon into the prepared loaf pans. Sprinkle with the Cinnamon-Sugar Topping. Bake for 50 to 60 minutes or until the bread tests done. Let stand to cool for 45 minutes. Remove to a wire rack to cool completely.

CINNAMON-SUGAR TOPPING

1 tablespoon all-purpose flour
5 tablespoons sugar

2 teaspoons ground cinnamon
1 tablespoon butter, softened

Combine the flour, sugar and cinnamon in a bowl and mix well. Add the butter and mix with a fork until crumbly.

Apple Pecan Cake

SERVES 20

1½ cups corn oil
2 cups sugar
2 eggs, beaten
2 teaspoons vanilla extract

3 cups chopped apples
1 cup chopped pecans
3 cups all-purpose flour
1 teaspoon baking soda

1 teaspoon salt
1 teaspoon ground cinnamon

Preheat the oven to 325 degrees. Grease five 3×5-inch foil loaf pans.

Beat the corn oil, sugar, eggs and vanilla extract in a mixing bowl until well mixed. Stir in the apples and pecans. Combine the flour, baking soda, salt and cinnamon in a bowl and mix well. Add to the apple mixture and mix well. Divide the batter evenly among the prepared loaf pans. Bake for 1 hour or until the loaves test done.

Note: *These loaves make nice holiday gifts for neighbors.*

Make-Ahead Cinnamon Rolls

SERVES 12

1 cup whole milk
10 tablespoons unsalted butter
  softened, divided
2 ½ teaspoons active dry yeast
3 ½ cups all-purpose flour
⅓ cup sugar

1 teaspoon salt
2 eggs
1 cup packed dark brown sugar
1 ½ tablespoons ground cinnamon
Cream Cheese Frosting (recipe below)

Combine the milk and 4 tablespoons of the butter in a large microwave-safe bowl or measuring cup. Microwave in 20-second increments just until the butter is melted; stir. Let the mixture stand to cool to 110 to 115 degrees on a candy thermometer. Stir in the yeast. Let stand for 3 to 5 minutes or until the yeast is activated and the mixture is foamy.

Combine the flour, sugar and salt in a mixing bowl. Beat with the paddle attachment just until mixed. Add the milk mixture gradually, beating constantly at low speed. Add the eggs. Beat at low speed for 3 to 4 minutes or until a soft ball forms, scraping the sides of the bowl occasionally.

Knead with the dough hook on low speed for 4 minutes or until the dough is soft, adding additional flour 1 tablespoon at a time if the dough is sticky.

Spray a large bowl with nonstick cooking spray or coat with canola oil. Place the dough in the bowl, turning to coat all sides. Cover with plastic wrap. Let rise in a warm place for 1 hour or until doubled in bulk.

Spread 2 tablespoons of the butter over the bottom and sides of a 9×13-inch glass baking dish. Roll the dough into a 16×20-inch rectangle on a floured surface. Spread evenly with the remaining 4 tablespoons butter. Sprinkle evenly with the brown sugar and cinnamon. Roll as for a jellyroll, starting at a short end. Cut into 12 even slices, arranging in the prepared baking dish. Let rise, loosely covered, for about 45 minutes. Chill, tightly covered, for 8 to 12 hours.

Let the rolls stand at room temperature for 30 minutes.

Preheat the oven to 350 degrees. Remove the Cream Cheese Frosting from the refrigerator. Bake the rolls for 15 to 20 minutes or until lightly browned. Drizzle or spread the frosting evenly over the warm rolls and serve.

CREAM CHEESE FROSTING

4 ounces cream cheese, softened
4 tablespoons unsalted butter,
  softened

1 ½ cups powdered sugar
1 teaspoon vanilla extract
⅛ teaspoon salt

Cream the cream cheese and butter in a mixing bowl. Beat in the powdered sugar, vanilla extract and salt, scraping the bowl if needed. Chill the frosting, covered, until ready to use.

Mixed Berry Crumb Cake

SERVES 6

2 ¼ cups all-purpose flour
3 teaspoons baking powder
1 teaspoon salt
1½ cups sugar
¼ cup shortening
1 cup milk

2 eggs
1½ teaspoons vanilla extract
1 cup fresh raspberries
1 cup fresh blackberries
1 cup fresh blueberries
Cinnamon Topping (recipe below)

Preheat the oven to 350 degrees. Grease and flour a 9×13-inch baking dish or cake pan.

Mix the flour, baking powder and salt in a medium bowl. Cream the sugar, shortening, milk, eggs and vanilla extract in a large mixing bowl. Add the flour mixture ½ cup at a time, beating well after each addition. Beat for 2 to 3 minutes or until smooth.

Spoon the batter into the prepared baking dish. Bake for 25 minutes or until the cake is set and the edges begin to turn golden brown.

Sprinkle the raspberries, blackberries and blueberries evenly over the warm cake, pressing lightly. Drop the Cinnamon Topping by marble-size pieces over the berries. Bake for 30 to 35 minutes longer or just until brown and crisp. Let stand to cool completely before serving.

CINNAMON TOPPING

2 cups butter, softened
3 cups all-purpose flour
⅔ cup sugar

⅔ cup brown sugar
1 tablespoon ground cinnamon
1 teaspoon vanilla extract

Combine the butter, flour, sugar, brown sugar, cinnamon and vanilla extract in a large bowl and mix well using hands.

Banana Muffins with Crumb Topping

MAKES 24

2 ¼ cups all-purpose flour
¾ teaspoon baking soda
½ teaspoon salt
¼ teaspoon ground cinnamon
2 eggs
½ cup vegetable oil
¾ cup sugar

4 to 5 medium very ripe bananas,
   mashed (about 2 cups)
¼ cup vanilla Greek yogurt
1½ teaspoons vanilla extract
1 cup chopped toasted walnuts
   (optional)
Crumb Topping (recipe below)

Preheat the oven to 350 degrees. Line 24 muffin cups with paper liners or grease the cups well.

Combine the flour, baking soda, salt and cinnamon in a bowl and mix well.

Beat the eggs and vegetable oil in a mixing bowl. Add the sugar and mix well. Beat in the bananas, yogurt and vanilla extract at medium speed until well mixed. Add the flour mixture and beat just until moistened. Stir in the walnuts.

Divide the batter evenly among the prepared muffin cups. Sprinkle with the Crumb Topping. Bake for 18 to 22 minutes or until the muffins test done, rotating the pans halfway through the baking time. Let stand to cool on a wire rack for 10 minutes. Remove from the muffin cups and serve.

CRUMB TOPPING

¾ cup all-purpose flour
½ cup powdered sugar
¼ cup packed brown sugar

½ teaspoon ground cinnamon
⅛ teaspoon salt
7 tablespoons butter, melted

Combine the flour, powdered sugar, brown sugar, cinnamon and salt in a bowl. Add the butter and mix with a fork until crumbs form, adding additional butter 1 tablespoon at a time if needed.

Warsaw Inn Polish Bread

SERVES 12

2 cups milk
4 tablespoons butter
2 tablespoons sugar
2 envelopes active dry yeast

2 teaspoons salt
2 eggs, divided
6¼ to 6¾ cups all-purpose flour
1 tablespoon water

Combine the milk and butter in a saucepan over medium-low heat. Heat to 110 to 115 degrees on a candy thermometer. Remove from the heat. Stir in the sugar, yeast, salt and 1 of the eggs. Let stand for 15 minutes or until bubbly.

Add enough of the flour to form a sticky dough. Knead on a lightly floured surface for 6 to 8 minutes or until stiff, smooth and elastic, adding as much of the remaining flour as needed. Shape into a ball.

Punch down the dough. Divide into halves. Let rise, covered, for 10 minutes.

Preheat the oven to 375 degrees. Grease two 8×12×2-inch or 9×5×3-inch loaf pans.

Place half of the dough in each prepared loaf pan, shaping into loaves. Let rise in a warm place for 30 minutes or until doubled in bulk.

Combine the remaining egg and water in a small bowl and mix well. Brush over the loaves. Bake for 25 to 30 minutes or until the loaves sound hollow. Cool in the pans on a wire rack for 10 to 15 minutes before removing.

Yuca Bread

MAKES 15 ROLLS

2 cups crumbled queso fresco
1¼ cups tapioca flour
1 tablespoon sugar
½ teaspoon baking powder

¼ teaspoon salt
4 tablespoons butter, softened
1 egg
4½ teaspoons heavy cream

Preheat the oven to 500 degrees. Line a large baking sheet with parchment paper.

Combine the queso fresco, flour, sugar, baking powder and salt in a large bowl and mix well.

Cut the butter into 4 to 6 slices. Add the butter, egg and cream to the cheese mixture and mix with hands until blended and shapeable.

Shape the dough into 1½-inch balls, arranging 2 inches apart on the prepared baking sheet. Bake for 6 to 7 minutes or until the dough has flattened slightly and is starting to turn golden brown. Serve warm or cool on a wire rack.

Homemade Everything Bagels

SERVES 6 TO 10

4 to 4¼ cups bread flour	2½ teaspoons instant yeast	Mixture of sesame seeds, poppy seeds,
4 tablespoons sugar, divided	12 ounces water, warmed to	coarse salt, dried minced garlic and
3 teaspoons salt	100-110 degrees	dried minced onion to taste

Whisk the flour, 3 tablespoons of the sugar and salt in a mixing bowl. Whisk in the yeast. Add the water in a slow steady stream, mixing with the dough hook at low speed. Mix at medium-high speed until a dough forms.

Knead the dough on a lightly floured surface until a smooth, slightly sticky dough forms, adding additional flour if needed. Shape into a ball. Let rise, covered with the mixing bowl, for 10 minutes.

Preheat the oven to 425 degrees. Line a few baking sheets with parchment paper.

Bring a large pot of water to a rolling boil and add the remaining 1 tablespoon sugar.

Divide the dough evenly into 6 to 10 pieces. Shape each piece into a 10- to 12-inch log. Wrap a log around palm of hand to form a donut shape, moisten one end with water, squeeze ends together and roll lightly on a flat surface to secure the ends. Repeat with the remaining logs.

Drop the bagels 3 at a time into the boiling water. Boil until the bagels rise to the top, using a slotted spoon to release from the bottom of the pot if needed. Remove to the prepared baking sheet. Sprinkle with the sesame seed mixture. Bake for 20 to 25 minutes or until puffed and golden brown. Let stand to cool slightly before serving.

Note: *This recipe uses instant yeast, not active dry yeast. Instant yeast does not need to bloom in water before being mixed with the dry ingredients. The salt and yeast should not be added at the same time. Be sure to mix the salt with the flour and sugar first and then add the yeast.*

Salads

Menu

Market to Table

Grilled Peaches with Whipped Ricotta Fig Toast ~ 24

Kale, Apple and Peanut Salad ~ 91

Summer Vegetable Ratatouille over Polenta ~ 200

Plum Strawberry Pie ~ 262

Healthy Habits

From 2008 to 2011, the Junior League of Denver developed and implemented the JLD Healthy Habits Program. League members provided a much-needed nutrition program to women and children living at Joshua Station, a local transitional housing facility. The program helped the families learn healthy nutrition and meal planning with workshops on topics such as shopping on a budget, healthy meal planning, healthy after-school snacks, and basic cooking skills.

Summer Salad with Watermelon Radishes

SERVES 8

1 head butter lettuce,
    leaves separated
1 small head radicchio,
    leaves separated
Marinated Feta (recipe below)
5 ounces baby kale, long stems
    removed

⅓ ounce fresh mint leaves
    (about 2 ½ tablespoons)
⅓ ounce fresh Italian parsley leaves
    (about 2 ½ tablespoons)
Flaky sea salt to taste
Pickled Radishes (recipe page 85)
Sections of 1 large orange
16 large blackberries, cut into halves

8 large strawberries, stemmed and
    cut into quarters
½ cup English peas (optional)
Strawberry Dressing (recipe below)
¼ to ½ cup edible flowers (such as
    chive, thyme, viola or kale blooms)
    (optional)

Place a leaf each of butter lettuce and radicchio on each of 8 salad plates.

Drain the Marinated Feta, reserving the marinade. Combine the kale, mint and parsley in a bowl. Add a small amount of the reserved marinade and toss to mix. Season with salt if desired. Divide the kale mixture evenly among the salads, making a nest on top of the lettuce.

Arrange the desired amount of the Pickled Radishes on each salad, reserving any remaining radishes in the refrigerator for another use. Divide the Marinated Feta, orange sections, blackberries, strawberries and peas evenly among the salads, arranging on and around the salad. Spoon the desired amount of Strawberry Dressing around the salads. Top with the edible flowers.

May layer the butter lettuce and radicchio on a large platter, spoon the kale mixture down the center, arrange the Marinated Feta, Pickled Radishes, orange sections, blackberries, strawberries, peas and edible flowers on and around the salad and serve the Strawberry Dressing on the side.

MARINATED FETA

1 (8-ounce) block feta cheese, cut into
    ½-inch squares

⅓ ounce fresh chives, finely chopped
    (about 2 ½ tablespoons)

¼ cup extra-virgin olive oil

Combine the feta cheese, chives and olive oil in a bowl. Chill, covered, for 8 to 12 hours, stirring occasionally.

STRAWBERRY DRESSING

8 ounces strawberries, stemmed
½ cup extra-virgin olive oil
¼ cup red raspberry vinegar

2 tablespoons rice vinegar
1 tablespoon honey
¼ teaspoon vanilla extract

Salt and freshly ground black pepper
    to taste

Combine the strawberries, olive oil, raspberry vinegar, rice vinegar, honey and vanilla extract in a blender and process until smooth. Season with salt and pepper.

PICKLED RADISHES

1 cup rice vinegar
1 cup water
½ ounce fresh ginger root, peeled and
    coarsely chopped
½ cup sugar

1 teaspoon mustard seeds
1 teaspoon coriander seeds
1 teaspoon salt
1 bay leaf

1 bunch Easter egg or red radishes,
    cut into quarters with tails intact
1 small unpeeled watermelon radish,
    thinly sliced

Combine the vinegar, water, ginger root, sugar, mustard seeds, coriander seeds, salt and bay leaf in a saucepan. Bring to a boil. Simmer until the sugar is dissolved, stirring occasionally. Chill, covered, until completely cooled.

Place the Easter egg radishes and watermelon radish in separate sealable containers. Strain the vinegar mixture. Add enough vinegar mixture to cover the radishes in each container. Chill, covered, for 15 minutes or up to 12 hours.

Arugula and Blueberry Salad with Citrus Vinaigrette

SERVES 4 TO 6

4 cups packed baby arugula, coarse
    stems removed
1 cup fresh blueberries
½ cup pistachios

½ cup thinly sliced scallions including
    green tops
Citrus Vinaigrette (recipe below)

Tear the arugula into bite-size pieces. Combine the arugula, blueberries, pistachios and scallions in a large bowl. Chill until serving time.

Pour a small amount of the Citrus Vinaigrette over the salad and toss to coat, adding additional vinaigrette if desired.

CITRUS VINAIGRETTE

½ cup walnut oil
2 teaspoons finely grated orange zest
1 teaspoon finely grated lemon zest
3 tablespoons fresh orange juice
3 tablespoons fresh lemon juice

1 tablespoon chopped fresh chives
1 teaspoon pure maple syrup
¼ teaspoon ground black pepper
¼ teaspoon kosher salt

Whisk the walnut oil, orange zest, lemon zest, orange juice, lemon juice, chives, maple syrup, pepper and salt in a small bowl.

Fennel and Radish Salad

SERVES 4 TO 6

1 cup thinly sliced fennel
1 head butter lettuce, coarsely
    chopped
½ head radicchio, coarsely chopped
4 green onions including green tops,
    coarsely chopped

15 red radishes, cut into ⅛-inch slices
1 pink grapefruit, cut into 1-inch
    pieces
¼ cup capers
Lemon Garlic Dressing (recipe below)

Cut the fennel into halves and then into ⅛-inch slices.

Combine the butter lettuce and radicchio in a medium bowl. Add the green onions, radishes, grapefruit, capers and fennel. Pour the Lemon Garlic Dressing over the salad and toss to mix. Serve immediately.

LEMON GARLIC DRESSING

½ cup extra-virgin olive oil
2 teaspoons lemon juice

1 clove garlic, minced
Salt and pepper to taste

Whisk the olive oil, lemon juice and garlic in a bowl. Season with the salt and pepper.

Entertaining Tip

For a unique and impressive table setting, try using unexpected items as place cards or menus. Write your menu on mini cutting boards, and they are adorable favors for your guests to take home. Wrap dinner rolls with paper name cards for beautiful and functional place markers.

Spring Salad with Asparagus

SERVES 4 TO 8

4 large eggs
12 ounces asparagus, cooked
  and chilled
2 cups packed arugula

4 slices red onion, chopped
1 bunch red radishes, sliced
4 ounces pecorino cheese, shaved
½ cup croutons

¼ cup extra-virgin olive oil
¼ cup red wine vinegar
1 teaspoon salt, or to taste
½ teaspoon pepper, or to taste

Combine the eggs with enough water to cover in a saucepan. Bring to a boil. Simmer for 12 minutes for hard-boiled eggs or 6 minutes for soft-boiled eggs; drain. Fill the saucepan with cold water to stop the cooking process. Break the egg shells all over and peel the eggs; if soft-boiled, the yolks should be barely cooked but not runny. Cut into slices.

Cut the asparagus into thirds. Arrange the asparagus, arugula, onion and radishes on a platter. Top with the pecorino cheese and croutons. Arrange the egg slices on or around the salad. Drizzle with the olive oil and vinegar. Season with the salt and pepper.

Fresh Colorado Salad with Avocado and Dates

SERVES 6 TO 8

10 ounces salad greens
4 medium chicken breasts, cooked
2 to 3 medium tomatoes, chopped
2 medium avocados, chopped

1 cup cooked fresh corn
1 cup dates, chopped
6 medium scallions, chopped
4 ounces crumbled goat cheese

Herb Dressing (recipe below)
1 cup croutons (such as corn bread
  croutons)
½ cup slivered almonds, toasted

Combine the salad greens, chicken, tomatoes, avocados, corn, dates, scallions and goat cheese in a salad bowl. Pour the desired amount of the Herb Dressing over the salad and toss to coat. Top with the croutons and almonds. Serve immediately.

HERB DRESSING

⅔ cup extra-virgin olive oil
⅓ cup lemon juice or white wine
  vinegar
3 tablespoons chopped fresh chives
3 tablespoons chopped fresh parsley

3 tablespoons chopped
  fresh tarragon
1 teaspoon salt
½ teaspoon pepper

Combine the olive oil, lemon juice, chives, parsley, tarragon, salt and pepper in a miniature food processor or blender and process until blended.

SPRING SALAD WITH ASPARAGUS

Kale, Apple and Peanut Salad

SERVES 4

2 bunches kale
2 large Granny Smith apples, cored
    and chopped
2 or 3 green onions, chopped

½ cup chopped peanuts
¼ cup chopped fresh cilantro
Peanut Dressing (recipe below)

Cut the kale into thin slices, resembling coleslaw. Place in a salad bowl. Add the apples, green onions, peanuts and cilantro and toss to mix. Pour the Peanut Dressing over the salad and toss to coat.

PEANUT DRESSING

¼ cup creamy peanut butter
Juice of 1 medium lime
2 tablespoons honey, or 1 tablespoon
    agave nectar
1 tablespoon extra-virgin olive oil

1 tablespoon rice wine vinegar
2 teaspoons soy sauce
1 teaspoon hot chili sauce
¼ teaspoon red pepper flakes
¼ cup water (optional)

Combine the peanut butter, lime juice, honey, olive oil, vinegar, soy sauce, chili sauce and red pepper flakes in a bowl and mix until blended. Add the water if needed for thinner consistency. May be made 24 hours in advance.

Entertaining Tip

To prolong the life of purchased flowers, simply keep the water in the vessel clean. This will slow bacteria buildup, which would make it difficult for the stems to hydrate. Ideally, the stems love a fresh cut with sharp scissors and fresh water every few days. It is also helpful to keep the blooms cool and away from direct sunlight.

Fall Squash Salad

SERVES 8

1 medium butternut squash
2 tablespoons extra-virgin olive oil
Salt and pepper to taste
1 tablespoon butter
3 small shallots, sliced
1 roasted chicken, shredded

4 cups mixed greens
6 ounces crumbled goat cheese
¼ cup dried cranberries or
   pomegranate seeds
Honey Mustard Dressing
   (recipe below)

Preheat the oven to 350 degrees.

Peel the squash and cut into ¾-inch pieces. Combine the squash, olive oil, salt and pepper in a bowl and toss to mix. Spread on a baking sheet. Bake for 45 to 60 minutes or until tender.

Melt the butter in a skillet over medium heat. Sauté the shallots in the butter until translucent. Remove from heat. Let stand to cool slightly. Combine the chicken, squash, greens, goat cheese and dried cranberries in a salad bowl. Pour the Honey Mustard Dressing over the salad and toss to coat.

HONEY MUSTARD DRESSING

½ cup extra-virgin olive oil
⅓ cup balsamic vinegar
2 tablespoons Dijon mustard

1 tablespoon honey
Salt and pepper to taste

Combine the olive oil, balsamic vinegar, mustard, honey, salt and pepper in a bowl and mix well.

Chicken and Gorgonzola Spinach Salad with Curry Dressing

SERVES 6

16 ounces fresh baby spinach
2 large chicken breasts, cooked
   and sliced
1 pound bacon, cooked and crumbled

6 ounces crumbled Gorgonzola cheese
4 large green onions
4 ounces slivered almonds
Curry Dressing (recipe below)

Combine the spinach, chicken, bacon, Gorgonzola cheese, green onions and almonds in a large salad bowl. Spoon the Curry Dressing over the salad and toss to coat.

CURRY DRESSING

½ cup mayonnaise
½ cup sour cream
1½ teaspoons curry powder

Combine the mayonnaise, sour cream and curry powder in a bowl and mix well. May be made ahead of time and chilled until serving time.

DISCOVER DENVER

In 1894, famous Titanic survivor Margaret "Molly" Brown and her husband, J.J., purchased a home in Denver's fashionable Capitol Hill neighborhood after making their fortune in gold mining. In 1970, to save the home from potential destruction, the Junior League of Denver provided funds to Historic Denver, Inc., as part of a down payment for purchase. Using photos taken during Mrs. Brown's occupancy, the home was restored to the opulence of turn-of-the-century Denver and opened as The Molly Brown House Museum, which still operates today. In the museum's early days, League members provided guided tours, conducted research, and helped cultivate collections.

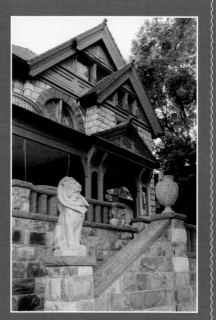

Thai Steak Salad

SERVES 6 TO 8

8 ounces rice noodles
1 teaspoon salt
Peanut oil or vegetable oil
12 to 16 ounces strip or sirloin steak, trimmed
Salt and pepper to taste
1 bunch salad greens and/or arugula

2 cups shredded green cabbage
1 large mango, peeled and chopped
1 cup cherry tomatoes, cut into halves
1 or 2 medium avocados, cut into bite-size pieces
2 medium carrots, shredded
½ cup fresh cilantro, chopped

½ cup fresh basil, chopped
¼ cup fresh mint leaves, chopped
2 medium scallions, chopped
Honey Lime Dressing (recipe below)
½ cup salted roasted peanuts, chopped

Cook the noodles with the salt according to the package directions until al dente; drain. Rinse with cold water; drain well. Toss the noodles with a small amount of peanut oil in a large salad bowl. Chill until serving time.

Preheat the grill to medium.

Season the steak with salt and pepper to taste. Grill to the desired degree of doneness. Cut into slices.

Add the steak, salad greens, cabbage, mango, cherry tomatoes, avocados, carrots, cilantro, basil, mint and scallions to the noodles. Pour the desired amount of the Honey Lime Dressing over the salad and toss to coat. Sprinkle with the peanuts and serve.

HONEY LIME DRESSING

¼ cup fresh lime juice
¼ cup peanut oil
2 tablespoons sesame oil
2 tablespoons hot chili sauce
1 tablespoon honey
1 clove garlic, minced
½ teaspoon minced fresh ginger
½ teaspoon salt

Combine the lime juice, peanut oil, sesame oil, chili sauce, honey, garlic, ginger and salt in a bowl and mix well. Chill until serving time.

Grilled Shrimp and Pineapple Salad

SERVES 6 TO 8

¼ cup shredded coconut
1 medium pineapple
1 pound shrimp, peeled and
    deveined, tails intact
4 cups mixed greens

Leaves of 1 head butter lettuce
¼ medium red onion, chopped
2 medium avocados, sliced
1 medium cucumber, chopped
Spicy Lime Dressing (recipe below)

Preheat the oven to 350 degrees. Spread the coconut on a baking sheet. Bake for 2 to 3 minutes or until lightly toasted.

Peel the pineapple and cut into 16 to 20 long slices. Thread the shrimp onto skewers. Heat a grill pan over medium heat or preheat a grill to medium. Grill the pineapple and shrimp for 3 to 4 minutes per side.

Divide the mixed greens, butter lettuce, shrimp, pineapple, onion, avocados and cucumber evenly among 6 to 8 salad plates. Drizzle each with a portion of the Spicy Lime Dressing. Sprinkle with the coconut and serve.

SPICY LIME DRESSING

¼ cup coconut oil
Juice of 1 lime
2 tablespoons whole grain mustard

1 tablespoon harissa
Salt to taste

Heat the coconut oil in a saucepan over low heat, or microwave just until liquefied. Combine the coconut oil, lime juice, mustard, harissa and salt in a bowl and mix well.

Chipotle Shrimp Cocktail

SERVES 6 TO 8

1 large red onion
1 medium red bell pepper
1 medium yellow bell pepper
2 pounds peeled, deveined large
   shrimp with tails removed, cooked

1 cup chili sauce
½ cup chopped fresh cilantro
½ cup fresh lime juice
½ cup fresh orange juice (such as
   blood orange juice)

2 or 3 canned chipotle peppers in
   adobo sauce, chopped

Cut the onion, red bell pepper and yellow bell pepper into thin strips. Combine the shrimp, onion and bell peppers in a large sealable plastic bag.

Whisk the chili sauce, cilantro, lime juice, orange juice and chipotle peppers in a bowl. Pour over the shrimp mixture. Chill for 12 to 24 hours, turning the bag occasionally. Spoon into martini glasses using a slotted spoon.

Farro Salad with Radishes, Arugula and Feta

SERVES 6 TO 8

1½ cups semi-pearled farro, rinsed
1 cup grape tomatoes, cut into halves
½ red onion, chopped
½ English cucumber, chopped
6 red radishes, cut into quarters
   or eighths

½ cup kalamata olives
¼ cup chopped fresh mint leaves
¼ cup chopped fresh Italian parsley
¼ cup extra-virgin olive oil
Juice of 1 lemon
2 cloves garlic, minced

⅛ teaspoon red pepper flakes
Kosher salt and black pepper to taste
2 cups baby arugula
¾ cup crumbled feta cheese
   (about 4 ounces)

Bring a large saucepan of salted water to a boil. Add the farro. Cook for 20 minutes or until tender; drain well. Let stand to cool slightly.

Combine the tomatoes, onion, cucumber, radishes, olives, mint and parsley in a large bowl. Combine the olive oil, lemon juice, garlic and red pepper flakes in a bowl and whisk until well mixed. Pour over the salad and stir to mix. Add the farro and mix well. Season with salt and pepper. Fold in the arugula and sprinkle with the feta cheese. Serve immediately.

Note: *If using whole grain farro, cook for 30 minutes or until tender.*

Cranberry and Pistachio Salad

SERVES 6 TO 8

1 cup instant couscous or quinoa
1 teaspoon salt
2 to 2½ cups orange juice, divided
1 cup dried cranberries
½ cup dried currants or golden raisins

1 cup chopped seeded English
   cucumber (optional)
1 medium scallion, chopped
½ cup coarsely chopped pistachios
¼ cup chopped fresh mint

2 tablespoons red wine vinegar
2 tablespoons extra-virgin olive oil
Salt and pepper to taste

Prepare the couscous or quinoa with the salt according to the package directions, using 1½ cups of the orange juice for the couscous or 2 cups of the orange juice for the quinoa. Fluff with a fork. Spoon into a large bowl.

Combine the dried cranberries, dried currants and ½ cup of the remaining orange juice in a saucepan. Bring to a boil. Let stand at room temperature for 15 minutes; drain.

Add the reconstituted fruit, cucumber, scallion, pistachios, mint, vinegar, olive oil, salt and pepper to the couscous and toss to mix. Serve at room temperature, or chill until serving time.

Southwest Quinoa Salad

SERVES 4 TO 6

4 medium ears corn, boiled
1½ cups quinoa, rinsed and drained
1 cup cherry tomatoes, cut into halves
1 (15-ounce) can black beans, rinsed
   and drained

1 medium red bell pepper, chopped
1 large cucumber, seeded and
   chopped
⅓ medium red onion, thinly sliced
¼ cup chopped fresh cilantro

Southwest Dressing (recipe below)
Leaves of 1 head butter lettuce,
   rinsed and patted dry
1 medium avocado, sliced

Cut the kernels from the corn into a bowl, scraping the cobs. Cook the quinoa according to the package directions. Let stand to cool. Combine the quinoa, corn, tomatoes, black beans, bell pepper, cucumber, onion and cilantro in a large bowl. Pour ½ cup or more of the Southwest Dressing over the salad and mix well. Arrange the lettuce in a circular pattern on a platter. Spoon the salad onto the center. Arrange the avocado on top.

SOUTHWEST DRESSING

½ cup extra-virgin olive oil
Juice of 1 lime
1 medium clove garlic, pressed

1 teaspoon ground cumin
1 teaspoon chili powder

½ teaspoon sea salt
⅛ teaspoon hot pepper sauce

Whisk the olive oil, lime juice, garlic, cumin, chili powder, sea salt and hot pepper sauce in a bowl until well blended.

BEET SALAD

Beet Salad

SERVES 6

10 to 12 medium beets with
    green tops
5 ounces baby spinach or mixed
    greens (about 4 cups)

3 clementines, sectioned
6 ounces crumbled goat cheese
½ cup walnuts, toasted
Shallot Vinaigrette (recipe below)

Cut off the tops and root ends of the beets, reserving any tender tops. Combine the beets and enough water to cover in a large saucepan. Bring to a boil. Boil for 20 minutes or until tender when pierced with a fork; drain. Let stand to cool slightly. Peel the beets under cool running water. Cut the beets and tender tops into bite-size pieces.

Divide the spinach, beets, beet tops, clementines, goat cheese and walnuts evenly among 4 salad plates. Drizzle each with 2 tablespoons of the Shallot Vinaigrette.

SHALLOT VINAIGRETTE

¼ cup walnut oil
3 tablespoons sherry vinegar

3 tablespoons minced shallots

Combine the walnut oil, vinegar and shallots in a bowl and whisk to mix well.

Blue Ribbon Potato Salad

SERVES 8 TO 10

2½ to 3 pounds red potatoes
6 ounces good-quality chunky blue
    cheese salad dressing
3 tablespoons sour cream
1½ teaspoons fresh coarsely ground
    black pepper

6 ounces crumbled blue cheese
2 (8-ounce) cans sliced water
    chestnuts, drained, slices
    cut into halves
½ cup thinly sliced green onions
Salt and pepper to taste

Scrub the potatoes and cut into bite-size pieces. Combine the potatoes and enough water to cover in a large pot. Bring to a boil. Simmer, covered, for 7 to 9 minutes or until tender but firm; drain. Add the salad dressing, sour cream and 1½ teaspoons pepper to the potatoes immediately and mix well. Let stand to cool for 30 to 45 minutes, stirring occasionally.

Reserve ½ cup of the blue cheese, chilling until serving time. Combine the potato mixture, water chestnuts, green onions and remaining blue cheese in a bowl and mix well. Season with salt and pepper to taste. Chill, covered, for up to 24 hours. Stir the salad and spoon into a serving bowl. Sprinkle with the reserved blue cheese.

Mediterranean Salad with Riced Cauliflower

SERVES 8

1 pound riced cauliflower, or ½ head
    cauliflower, riced (see Note)
½ cup grated Parmesan cheese
2 medium tomatoes, chopped

1 medium cucumber, chopped
1 medium yellow or red bell pepper,
    chopped
6 slices red onion, minced

½ cup kalamata olives, cut into halves
1 (15-ounce) can chick-peas, drained
Mediterranean Dressing
    (recipe below)

Combine the cauliflower, Parmesan cheese, tomatoes, cucumber, bell pepper, onion, olives and chick-peas in a large salad bowl. Pour the Mediterranean Dressing over the salad and toss to coat. Garnish with sprigs of fresh thyme or oregano.

MEDITERRANEAN DRESSING

½ cup extra-virgin olive oil
2 tablespoons lemon juice
2 cloves garlic

1 teaspoon salt
½ teaspoon red pepper flakes
½ teaspoon dried oregano

½ teaspoon dried basil
½ teaspoon dried thyme

Combine the olive oil, lemon juice, garlic, salt, red pepper flakes, oregano, basil and thyme in a food processor or blender. Process until the garlic is finely chopped and the mixture is blended.

Note: *To make riced cauliflower, pulse raw cauliflower florets in batches in a food processor until broken into rice-size pieces.*

Moroccan Orange Salad

SERVES 4 TO 6

3 to 4 blood oranges
3 to 4 large oranges

1 tablespoon orange blossom water
2½ tablespoons powdered sugar

1 teaspoon ground cinnamon

Peel the oranges including the white pith, using a serrated knife and working over a bowl. Cut the oranges into slices, discarding any seeds.

Arrange the oranges on a platter. Sprinkle with the orange blossom water and powdered sugar. Let stand for 20 to 30 minutes. Sprinkle with the cinnamon just before serving.

Note: *This salad may also be served as a dessert after a rich meal.*

MEDITERRANEAN SALAD

SPIRALIZED APPLE SALAD

Spiralized Apple Salad with Citrus Dressing

SERVES 4 TO 6

2 large red apples (such as Honeycrisp, Pink Lady or Gala)
2 large Granny Smith apples

Citrus Dressing (recipe below)
4 ounces sharp white Cheddar cheese, cut into ¼-inch cubes

⅔ cup pecan halves
½ cup dried cranberries
2 tablespoons sunflower seeds

Cut the red apples and Granny Smith apples into spirals using a spiralizer, or cut into julienne, working in batches. Place in a large bowl or individual bowls, drizzling each batch with a small amount of the Citrus Dressing to prevent browning.

Add the Cheddar cheese, pecans, dried cranberries and sunflower seeds to the apples and toss to mix.

Whisk the Citrus Dressing. Pour over the salad and toss to coat. Serve immediately.

CITRUS DRESSING

6 tablespoons extra-virgin olive oil
2 tablespoons lemon juice
Grated zest of 1 lemon

2 tablespoons orange juice
Grated zest of 1 orange
1½ teaspoons honey

¼ teaspoon kosher salt
Black pepper to taste

Combine the olive oil, lemon juice, lemon zest, orange juice, orange zest and honey in a jar or blender. Shake until well mixed, or process for 10 seconds or until blended. Season with salt and pepper.

Watermelon Salad

SERVES 4 TO 6

7½ cups cubed watermelon (1-inch cubes)
¼ medium red onion, chopped
1 cup crumbled feta cheese

¼ cup chopped fresh basil
¼ cup extra-virgin olive oil
2 tablespoons balsamic vinegar

Combine the watermelon, onion, feta cheese, basil and olive oil in a shallow salad bowl and toss to mix. Chill until serving time. Drizzle with the balsamic vinegar; do not toss. Serve immediately.

Pizza & Pasta

Menu

A Slice of Fun

SUMMER

Ginger Fizzy Drink ~ 54

Cannoli Fruit Dip ~ 42

Mini Pizzas ~ 115

Orange Olive Oil Cupcakes ~ 253

A Museum for Children

In 1975, the Junior League of Denver adopted the newly created A Museum for Children (now known as the Children's Museum of Denver at Marsico Campus) as a two-year community project. JLD volunteers organized classes and workshops for children, created and staffed a specialty gift shop, helped organize a benefit event, and awarded a grant to the museum. In the mid-1980s, the League once again got involved with the museum at its new location along the Platte River. League volunteers worked in partnership with museum staff to design and test a comprehensive volunteer program. Today, after a large expansion in 2015, the Children's Museum of Denver at Marsico Campus contains more than nine acres of hands-on exhibits where children can learn through play.

Sausage, Fig and Gorgonzola Pizza

SERVES 4

1 tablespoon extra-virgin olive oil
Classic Pizza Dough (recipe below)
1 large yellow onion, cut into thin
  slices
1 tablespoon butter
8 ounces ground hot Italian sausage
¼ cup fig preserves

¼ cup crumbled Gorgonzola cheese
8 ounces fresh mozzarella cheese,
  torn into bite-size pieces
Cajun or Creole seasoning to taste
  (optional)
Salt and pepper to taste (optional)

Preheat the oven to 450 degrees. Spread the olive oil over the bottom and sides of a 13×18-inch baking pan using a paper towel or pastry brush.

Punch down the Classic Pizza Dough a few times. Press over the bottom of the prepared baking pan. Bake for 6 minutes, pricking with a fork to release air if needed.

Sauté the onion in the butter in a skillet over medium-high heat just until tender, adding a small amount of water if needed to prevent overbrowning. Add the sausage. Cook until the sausage is browned, stirring to crumble; drain.

Spread the fig preserves over the pizza crust. Layer evenly with the sausage mixture, Gorgonzola cheese and mozzarella cheese. Season with Cajun seasoning or salt and pepper. Bake for 15 minutes or until the crust and cheeses begin to brown. Let stand to cool for 10 minutes before slicing.

CLASSIC PIZZA DOUGH

1 cup hot water
2¼ teaspoons active dry yeast
2 tablespoons extra-virgin olive oil

2½ to 3½ cups unbleached
  all-purpose flour, divided
Garlic salt to taste

Combine the hot water, yeast, olive oil, 2½ cups of the flour and garlic salt in the order listed in a mixing bowl. Mix at low speed using a dough hook until the dough pulls away from the sides of the bowl and does not stick to your fingers when touched, adding additional flour 1 tablespoon at a time if needed. Knead the dough a few times on a lightly floured surface, shaping into a ball. Place in a bowl sprayed with nonstick cooking spray. Cover with a clean kitchen towel. Let stand to rise in a warm, dry place for 1 hour.

Onion, Mushroom and Olive Pizza with White Sauce

SERVES 4

1 tablespoon extra-virgin olive oil
½ cup sliced onion
½ cup sliced mushrooms

1 pound pizza dough, at room temperature

1 cup White Sauce for Pizza (recipe page 118)
¼ cup sliced kalamata olives

Preheat the oven to 400 degrees, placing a pizza stone, pizza pan or baking sheet on the center rack.

Heat the olive oil in a skillet over medium-high heat. Sauté the onion and mushrooms in the hot oil for 10 minutes or until the mushrooms are browned. Remove from the heat.

Press or roll the dough into a ⅛-inch-thick circle on a piece of parchment paper and transfer the paper to the preheated pizza stone or pan. Spread with the White Sauce for Pizza. Spoon the onion mixture evenly over the sauce. Sprinkle with the olives. Bake for 10 to 15 minutes or until done to taste.

Grilled Pizza

SERVES 4

2 tablespoons cornmeal
1 pound pizza dough, at room temperature
3 Roma tomatoes

8 ounces fresh mozzarella cheese in water, drained
½ cup (about) extra-virgin olive oil, divided

1 cup loosely packed basil leaves, chopped

Preheat the grill to medium. Sprinkle the cornmeal evenly over a 9×13-inch baking sheet.

Stretch the dough into a rectangle on a lightly floured surface. Transfer to the prepared baking sheet and stretch into one 9×13-inch rectangle or two smaller rectangles.

Cut the tomatoes into thin slices and arrange in a single layer on a paper towel–lined plate. Cut the mozzarella cheese into thin slices and arrange in a single layer on a paper towel–lined plate. Pat the tomatoes and cheese dry using paper towels.

Brush the dough lightly with olive oil. Place oil side down on the grill rack, removing carefully from the baking sheet. Grill, covered, for 2 minutes. Prick with a fork to release air if needed. Transfer carefully to the baking sheet using a large spatula. Brush the top of the dough lightly with olive oil. Place oil side down on the grill rack, removing carefully from the baking sheet. Arrange the tomatoes, mozzarella cheese and basil on top of the dough, working quickly. Grill, covered, for 2 minutes. Remove to a cutting board and slice.

Prosciutto and Arugula Pizza with Pesto

SERVES 4

1 pound pizza dough, at room
  temperature
2 tablespoons extra-virgin olive oil,
  divided
1 tablespoon Italian seasoning
3 tablespoons pesto
8 ounces shredded mozzarella cheese

8 ounces shredded Parmesan cheese
2 ounces prosciutto, torn into
  bite-size pieces
2 cups baby arugula
Juice of 1 large lemon
Salt and pepper to taste

Preheat the oven to 400 degrees, placing a pizza stone, pizza pan or baking sheet on the center rack.

Press or roll the dough into a ⅛-inch-thick circle on a piece of parchment paper and transfer the paper to the preheated pizza stone or pan. Spread 1 tablespoon of the olive oil over the dough. Sprinkle evenly with the Italian seasoning. Spread with the pesto. Layer with half the mozzarella cheese, half the Parmesan cheese, prosciutto, remaining mozzarella cheese and remaining Parmesan cheese. Bake for 20 to 25 minutes or until the cheese is melted and the dough is dark brown.

Place the arugula in a medium bowl. Add the remaining 1 tablespoon olive oil, lemon juice, salt and pepper and toss to coat. Arrange evenly over the pizza. Cut into slices and serve immediately.

Note: *May shave additional Parmesan cheese over the pizza just before serving. May serve as a main dish or an appetizer.*

Entertaining Tip

Serve up "A Slice of Fun" by throwing a pizza party! Get your guests involved and have them create their own personalized pies. Provide a variety of topping options like classic mozzarella, tomatoes, and basil, along with figs, Gorgonzola cheese, fresh greens, and Italian meats for more gourmet tastes.

Pizza Tarts

SERVES 4 TO 6

1 (17-ounce) package frozen
　puff pastry, thawed
1 cup tomato purée
2 cloves garlic, minced
1 teaspoon dried oregano
⅛ teaspoon sugar
Salt and pepper to taste
½ cup thinly sliced red onion

2 tablespoons extra-virgin olive oil
1 tablespoon balsamic vinegar or red
　wine vinegar
1 cup feta cheese crumbles
½ cup kalamata olives, pitted and cut
　into quarters
¼ cup roasted red peppers

Preheat the oven to 425 degrees. Line 2 large baking sheets with parchment paper.

Roll each sheet of the puff pastry into a 12-inch square on a lightly floured surface. Cut each square into halves and place on the prepared baking sheets. Brush a small amount of water around a ½-inch border of each of the 4 halves. Fold in the borders ¼ inch to form an edge.

Combine the tomato purée, garlic, oregano, sugar, salt and pepper in a bowl and mix well. Combine the onion, olive oil and vinegar in a bowl and toss to coat. Let stand for 5 minutes; drain.

Divide the tomato sauce evenly among the puff pastry squares, spreading to the edge. Sprinkle with the feta cheese, onion, olives and roasted red peppers. Bake for 18 to 22 minutes or until the crust is golden brown. Let stand to cool for 5 minutes before cutting into rectangles. May be served warm or at room temperature.

DISCOVER DENVER

Cheesman Park, what we know today as a beautiful tree-lined urban green space, famously began its life as Mount Prospect Cemetery. When the city received approval to convert the cemetery to park space in 1890, the contract to move the "residents" to a new location went to an undertaker named E.P. McGovern. He was dismissed after accusations of mishandling and corruption, allegedly before the job was completed. This makes Cheesman Park a popular stop for both residents and ghost hunters alike!

Mini Pizzas

MAKES 20

1½ cups whole wheat flour or
  all-purpose flour
2⅔ cups all-purpose flour, divided
3⅓ teaspoons fast-rising active
  dry yeast
1½ teaspoons salt
1½ cups warm water
  (125 to 130 degrees)
3 tablespoons (or more) light olive oil

Cornmeal
1 cup pizza sauce
1 to 2 cups shredded mozzarella
  cheese
1 to 2 cups toppings (such as spinach,
  bell peppers, mushrooms,
  pepperoni, black olives and basil)
20 teaspoons grated Parmesan
  cheese

Combine the whole wheat flour, 1⅓ cups of the all-purpose flour, yeast and salt in a large bowl and mix well. Add the warm water and 3 tablespoons olive oil and stir until well blended. Stir in the remaining 1⅓ cups all-purpose flour. Stir until the dough forms a ball and pulls away from the sides of the bowl.

Knead the dough on a lightly floured surface for 5 minutes or until smooth and elastic. Divide the dough into 20 pieces and shape into smooth balls. Cover with a bowl or clean kitchen towel. Let stand to rest for 10 minutes.

Preheat the oven to 450 degrees. Sprinkle a small amount of cornmeal over baking sheets or 20 mini pizza pans.

Roll or shape the dough into flat crusts and place on the prepared baking sheets or pizza pans. Brush lightly with olive oil. Spread with the pizza sauce. Add the mozzarella cheese and toppings; do not overcrowd the pizza crusts or the crusts will become soggy. Bake for 10 minutes or until the cheese begins to brown and the crusts are crispy. Let stand to rest for a few minutes. Sprinkle with the Parmesan cheese.

Individual Beet and Pistachio Flat Breads

SERVES 4

3 medium beets, trimmed

4 (6×11-inch) flat breads

¼ cup jellied cranberry sauce

Grated zest and juice of
   1 large orange

2 tablespoons well-stirred tahini

1 teaspoon minced fresh garlic

½ teaspoon freshly ground pepper,
   or to taste

½ teaspoon red pepper flakes

4 ounces goat cheese, crumbled

⅓ cup pistachios, coarsely chopped

2 tablespoons sesame seeds,
   lightly toasted

1 teaspoon kosher salt, or to taste

1 cup snipped watercress leaves or
   other microgreens

Preheat the oven to 375 degrees.

Wrap the beets in foil. Roast for 45 to 60 minutes. Let stand to cool. Peel the beets and chop to make 3 cups.

Bake the flat breads according to the package directions. Maintain oven temperature.

Combine the beets, cranberry sauce, orange zest, orange juice, tahini, garlic, pepper and red pepper flakes in a food processor or blender. Pulse until well mixed but grainy. Divide evenly among the flat breads, spreading and leaving a small border. Sprinkle each with 1 ounce of the goat cheese. Bake until the flat breads are crisp and the cheese is melted. Sprinkle with the pistachios, sesame seeds and salt. Top each with ¼ cup of the watercress. Season with additional salt and pepper if needed. Serve immediately.

Cauliflower Pizza Crust

SERVES 4

1 pound riced cauliflower (see Note)
½ teaspoon salt
½ cup grated Parmesan cheese
1 egg

2 teaspoons Italian seasoning
½ teaspoon salt
½ teaspoon pepper

Combine the cauliflower and salt with enough water to cover in a medium saucepan. Bring to a boil. Boil for 3 to 4 minutes; drain through a mesh strainer. Press out any excess moisture with a flour sack towel or cheesecloth.

Preheat the oven to 450 degrees, placing a pizza stone on the center rack.

Combine the cauliflower, Parmesan cheese, egg, Italian seasoning, salt and pepper in a bowl and mix well. Spread ⅓ inch thick directly on the preheated pizza stone. Bake for 30 minutes. Add desired sauce, cheese and toppings and bake for 10 minutes or until the cheese is bubbly and brown. Let stand to cool slightly before cutting.

Note: *To make riced cauliflower, pulse raw cauliflower florets in batches in a food processor until broken into rice-size pieces.*

White Sauce for Pizza

SERVES 8

2 tablespoons butter
1 tablespoon extra-virgin olive oil
3 tablespoons minced garlic
⅓ cup minced onion
3 tablespoons all-purpose flour
1 cup milk

½ teaspoon salt
½ teaspoon ground pepper
¼ teaspoon dried oregano
¼ teaspoon dried basil
½ cup shredded Parmigiano-Reggiano
   cheese

Heat the butter and olive oil in a saucepan over medium heat until the butter is melted. Add the garlic and onion. Cook for 10 minutes or until tender, stirring occasionally. Add the flour. Cook for 1 minute, stirring constantly. Stir in the milk, salt, pepper, oregano and basil. Cook for 1 minute, stirring frequently. Add the Parmigiano-Reggiano cheese. Cook for 2 to 3 minutes or until the cheese is melted, stirring constantly.

Mac and Cheese with Gruyère, Peas and Pea Shoots

SERVES 4

8 ounces rigatoni
2 tablespoons butter, softened
2 tablespoons all-purpose flour
1 cup whole milk
Salt and pepper to taste
½ cup shredded Gruyère cheese
2 ounces shredded mozzarella cheese

1½ ounces pea shoots, cut into 1-inch
  pieces
1 cup green peas
1 tablespoon grated pecorino cheese
3 tablespoons panko
1 tablespoon coarsely chopped fresh
  parsley

Preheat the oven to 450 degrees, placing one oven rack at the top position and one at the bottom position.

Cook the rigatoni according to the package directions just until al dente; drain.

Knead the butter and flour together in a small bowl until smooth to make a beurre manié. Cook the milk in a saucepan over medium-high heat for 2 to 3 minutes or just until bubbles begin to form. Add the beurre manié 1 teaspoon at a time, stirring after each addition. Cook for 1 minute or until the mixture is smooth, whisking constantly. Remove from the heat. Season with salt and pepper. Add the Gruyère cheese, mozzarella cheese, pea shoots, peas and rigatoni and stir to mix. Spoon into a 9×9-inch baking dish. Sprinkle with the pecorino cheese and panko. Cover loosely with foil.

Bake on the top oven rack for 5 minutes or just until bubbly; remove the foil. Move to the bottom oven rack. Bake for 5 to 7 minutes or until cooked through. Let stand to cool for 5 minutes. Sprinkle with the parsley.

In the early 2000s, the Junior League of Denver, along with Leagues in 225 cities across the US, initiated the Kids in the Kitchen program. Recognizing that obesity can affect the health and well-being of children in their communities, these Leagues developed programming to educate children and their families about the importance of nutrition and fitness through hands-on experiences.

Horseradish Mac and Cheese

SERVES 4

8 ounces rotini
6 tablespoons butter
¼ cup all-purpose flour
2 cups whole milk

2 ½ cups shredded horseradish-flavor
    Cheddar cheese, divided
1 ½ cups shredded Gruyère cheese

12 ounces kielbasa, chopped and
    browned
1 cup crushed pretzels

Bring a large pot of salted water to a boil. Add the rotini. Cook until al dente; drain, reserving 1 cup of the pasta water.

Preheat the oven to 400 degrees.

Melt the butter in a saucepan over medium heat. Whisk in the flour. Cook for 1 minute, whisking constantly. Add the milk gradually, whisking constantly. Cook until the sauce is smooth, whisking constantly. Add 2 cups of the Cheddar cheese and Gruyère cheese. Stir in the rotini and enough of the reserved pasta water until the desired consistency is reached.

Spoon into a baking dish. Add the remaining ½ cup Cheddar cheese and kielbasa and stir gently. Sprinkle with the pretzels. Bake for 15 minutes.

Chicken Bow Tie Pasta

SERVES 8

2 chicken breasts
16 ounces farfalle
½ cup chopped celery
½ cup chopped red bell pepper
½ cup chopped pecans
¼ cup chopped fresh parsley

1 ½ tablespoons chopped
    green onions
½ teaspoon dried dill weed
½ teaspoon celery seeds
¼ teaspoon Cajun or Creole
    seasoning

⅛ teaspoon black pepper
Salt to taste
½ cup mayonnaise
2 tablespoons red wine vinegar
1 tablespoon lemon juice
1 ½ teaspoons extra-virgin olive oil

Preheat the oven to 375 degrees.

Place the chicken in a baking dish. Bake for 45 minutes or until cooked through. Let stand to cool slightly. Chop the chicken.

Cook the farfalle according to the package directions; drain.

Combine the chicken, farfalle, celery, bell pepper, pecans, parsley, green onions, dill weed, celery seeds, Cajun seasoning, pepper and salt in a bowl and mix well. Mix the mayonnaise, vinegar, lemon juice and olive oil in a bowl. Add to the chicken mixture and toss to coat. Chill, covered, until serving time.

HORSERADISH MAC AND CHEESE

Chicken Gorgonzola Penne

SERVES 4

---

2 medium chicken breasts
Vegetable oil for coating
Salt and pepper to taste
10 ounces penne
2 tablespoons chopped yellow onion
2 tablespoons chopped garlic

1½ teaspoons extra-virgin olive oil
2 ounces white wine
1¼ cups heavy cream
4 ounces Parmesan cheese, grated
5 ounces Gorgonzola cheese, or to taste, crumbled

1 cup seedless red grapes, cut into halves
½ cup walnuts, chopped
2 ounces fresh parsley, chopped
Parmesan Crisps (recipe below)

Preheat the grill to medium-high.

Coat the chicken with a small amount of vegetable oil and season with salt and pepper. Grill for 5 to 6 minutes per side or to 165 degrees on a meat thermometer. Remove to a cutting board. Let stand to rest for a few minutes. Cut into slices.

Cook the penne according to the package directions until al dente; drain.

Sauté the onion and garlic in the olive oil in a skillet until the onion is translucent. Add the wine and stir to deglaze the skillet. Stir in the cream and Parmesan cheese. Cook until thick enough to coat the back of the spoon, stirring frequently. Add the penne. Cook until heated through. Add the Gorgonzola cheese, grapes and walnuts and toss to mix. Divide the pasta mixture and chicken evenly among 4 pasta bowls. Top each with equal portions of the parsley and Parmesan Crisps.

PARMESAN CRISPS

---

2 ounces Parmesan cheese

Preheat the oven to 350 degrees. Line a baking sheet with a silicone mat or parchment paper.

Grate the Parmesan cheese into 2-inch diameter piles on the prepared baking sheet and pat lightly, or slice the cheese thinly and arrange on the baking sheet. Bake for 5 minutes or until golden brown and crisp.

Baked Pasta with Tomatoes, Shiitake Mushrooms and Prosciutto

SERVES 6 TO 8

2 cups finely chopped onions
2 large cloves garlic, minced
¼ teaspoon hot red pepper flakes
1 teaspoon dried basil, crumbled
1 teaspoon dried oregano, crumbled
2 tablespoons extra-virgin olive oil
1 pound shiitake mushroom caps, stemmed and sliced
4 tablespoons unsalted butter, divided

3 tablespoons all-purpose flour
2 cups milk
2 (28-ounce) cans Italian tomatoes, well drained and chopped
4 ounces thinly sliced prosciutto, cut into strips
4 ounces Italian fontina cheese, grated
4 ounces Gorgonzola cheese, crumbled

1½ cups freshly grated Parmesan cheese, divided
½ cup minced fresh parsley
16 ounces farfalle or penne
Salt and pepper to taste

Cook the onions, garlic, red pepper flakes, basil and oregano in the olive oil in a large skillet over medium-low heat until the onions are tender, stirring frequently. Add the mushrooms. Cook over medium heat for 10 to 15 minutes or until the mushrooms are tender, stirring constantly. Remove to a large bowl.

Melt 3 tablespoons of the butter in the skillet drippings over medium-low heat. Whisk in the flour. Cook for 3 minutes, stirring constantly. Add the milk in a steady stream, whisking constantly. Cook for 2 minutes or until thickened, whisking constantly. Pour over the mushroom mixture. Add the tomatoes, prosciutto, fontina cheese, Gorgonzola cheese, 1¼ cups of the Parmesan cheese and parsley.

Preheat the oven to 450 degrees, moving the oven rack to the center position. Butter a 3- to 4-quart baking dish.

Cook the farfalle in enough boiling water to cover in a saucepan for 5 minutes (pasta will not be tender); drain. Add the farfalle, salt and pepper to the tomato mixture and toss to mix. Spoon into the prepared baking dish. May prepare the dish to this point and chill, covered, for 8 to 12 hours. Bring to room temperature.

Sprinkle the remaining ¼ cup Parmesan cheese over the pasta and dot with the remaining 1 tablespoon butter. Bake for 25 to 30 minutes or until the farfalle is tender and the Parmesan cheese is golden brown.

Stuffed Shells with Red and White Sauces

SERVES 6 TO 8

1 (10-ounce) package frozen chopped spinach, thawed
2 tablespoons extra-virgin olive oil
¼ cup chopped onion
2 cloves garlic, minced
¼ teaspoon freshly grated nutmeg
1 pound ground beef

2 eggs, lightly beaten
2 tablespoons heavy cream
¼ cup plus 5 teaspoons freshly grated Parmigiano-Reggiano cheese, divided
¼ cup (about) chopped Italian parsley
1 teaspoon (about) sea salt

1 teaspoon (about) cracked black pepper
½ teaspoon dried oregano
Red and White Sauces (recipe below)
1 (12-ounce) package jumbo pasta shells

Drain the spinach and squeeze dry. Chop the spinach. Heat the olive oil in a skillet over medium heat. Cook the onion and garlic in the hot olive oil for 7 to 8 minutes or until tender; do not overbrown. Stir in the nutmeg. Add the ground beef. Cook until browned, stirring to crumble. Stir in the spinach. Cook for 3 to 4 minutes or until all of the moisture has evaporated and the spinach starts to stick to the skillet.

Combine the eggs, cream, 5 teaspoons of the Parmigiano-Reggiano cheese, parsley, sea salt, black pepper and oregano in a small bowl and mix well. Stir into the spinach mixture. Season with additional sea salt and black pepper if needed.

Preheat the oven to 350 degrees. Spread a thin layer of the Red Sauce in a 9×13-inch glass baking dish.

Cook the pasta shells according to the package directions for 20 minutes or just until al dente; drain. Stuff the shells with the spinach mixture, arranging in a single layer in the prepared baking dish. Pour the White Sauce evenly over the shells, covering completely. Spoon the remaining Red Sauce over the shells. Sprinkle the remaining ¼ cup Parmigiano-Reggiano cheese over the top. Bake for 25 to 35 minutes or until hot and bubbly. Sprinkle with additional Italian parsley.

RED AND WHITE SAUCES

1 cup chopped onion
4 to 5 cloves garlic, minced
3 tablespoons extra-virgin olive oil
4 cups tomato purée
2 teaspoons sugar

1 teaspoon dried basil
Salt and pepper to taste
4 tablespoons unsalted butter
¼ cup all-purpose flour
1 cup whole or 2-percent milk

1 cup heavy cream
½ teaspoon freshly grated nutmeg
White pepper to taste

For the Red Sauce, cook the onion and garlic in the olive oil in a 3-quart saucepan over medium heat for 7 to 8 minutes or until tender; do not burn. Stir in the tomato purée, sugar and basil. Season with salt and pepper to taste. Simmer, partially covered, for 40 minutes.

For the White Sauce, melt the butter in a 2-quart saucepan over medium heat. Sprinkle with the flour. Cook for 3 minutes, stirring constantly. Add the milk gradually, stirring constantly and breaking up any lumps. Bring to a simmer. Stir in the cream, nutmeg, salt and white pepper. Cook just until heated through; do not boil.

Creole Sausage Linguini

SERVES 6

8 ounces linguini
2 (14-ounce) packages Polish sausage
    or kielbasa, thinly sliced
1 tablespoon extra-virgin olive oil
1 medium red bell pepper, chopped
1 bunch scallions including light green
    tops, chopped
2 to 3 cloves garlic, minced

2 teaspoons Cajun or Creole
    seasoning, or to taste
¼ teaspoon crushed red pepper
    flakes, or to taste
1 cup heavy whipping cream
½ cup grated Parmesan cheese
    (optional)

Cook the linguini according to the package directions; drain.

Sauté the sausage in the olive oil in a skillet over medium-high heat until cooked through. Reduce the heat to medium. Add the bell pepper and scallions. Sauté until tender; drain. Stir in the garlic, Cajun seasoning and red pepper flakes. Cook for 1 minute, stirring occasionally.

Add the cream a few tablespoons at a time until the desired consistency is reached. Cook until heated through, stirring occasionally. Add the Parmesan cheese to thicken the sauce if desired. Serve with the linguini.

Entertaining Tip

When selecting blooms from a grocery store or florist to create your own arrangements, try purchasing ten to twenty stems of all one flower type in one color. Trim the stems to your desired length and put them in a vessel that is proportionate to the length of the stem. The simplicity of a monochromatic arrangement is always stylish. Take one stem and place in a bud vase or a small glass jar for your powder room for a coordinating and pretty detail.

Linguini with Sautéed Butternut Squash and Garlic

SERVES 8

4 cups butternut squash, peeled and cut into ½-inch pieces
4 cloves garlic, minced
⅓ cup extra-virgin olive oil
16 ounces linguini

Kosher salt and finely ground black pepper to taste
1 tablespoon chopped Italian parsley
Shredded Provolone cheese to taste

Sauté the squash and garlic in the olive oil in a large skillet over medium-low heat for 25 minutes or until the squash is tender.

Cook the linguini according to the package directions; drain. Add to the squash mixture and toss to mix. Season with salt.

Divide the linguini mixture evenly among 4 pasta bowls. Sprinkle with pepper, parsley and Provolone cheese. Serve immediately. May serve with heirloom tomatoes mixed with olive oil, minced garlic, dried oregano, salt and pepper. May substitute quinoa, rice or gluten-free pasta for the linguini.

Note: *The squash mixture may be used as a pizza topping. Just add fresh mozzarella cheese and bake at 400 degrees for 10 minutes. Drizzle with olive oil and sprinkle with chopped fresh parsley.*

DISCOVER DENVER

To coincide with the 2008 Democratic National Convention, Denver introduced a pioneering bike-sharing program, now known as B-cycle, to help provide transportation for locals and visitors in downtown Denver.

Muffaletta Pasta Salad

SERVES 10

1½ cups pimiento-stuffed green
   olives, chopped
1 cup kalamata olives, pitted and
   chopped
¼ cup olive juice
1 cup drained giardiniera, chopped
¾ cup Italian parsley, chopped
⅔ cup extra-virgin olive oil

2 tablespoons non-pareil capers
1 teaspoon anchovy paste
2 cloves garlic, minced
Crushed red pepper flakes to taste
1 pound gnocchetti, campanelle or
   similar pasta
4 ounces mortadella, thinly sliced and
   julienned

4 ounces Italian salami, thinly sliced
   and julienned
2 ounces prosciutto, thinly sliced and
   julienned
4 ounces provolone cheese, thinly
   sliced and julienned

Combine the green olives, kalamata olives, olive juice, giardiniera, parsley, olive oil, capers, anchovy paste, garlic and red pepper flakes in a large bowl or sealable plastic bag and mix well. Chill, covered or sealed, for 8 to 12 hours.

Cook the gnocchetti according to the package directions until al dente; drain. Place in a large bowl. Add the olive mixture immediately. Let stand to cool to room temperature, stirring occasionally.

Add the mortadella, salami, prosciutto and provolone cheese to the pasta mixture and toss to mix. Garnish with additional salami slices and whole olives. Garnish with sprigs of fresh parsley.

Summer-Style Orzo Salad

SERVES 8

1 pound orzo
½ cup extra-virgin olive oil
¼ cup red wine vinegar
Juice of 2 lemons
1 tablespoon Dijon mustard
Salt and pepper to taste
1 cup red cherry tomatoes, cut into halves
1 cup yellow cherry tomatoes, cut into halves
5 ounces feta cheese, crumbled
½ cup pine nuts, toasted
2 tablespoons fresh basil chiffonade

Cook the orzo according to the package directions until al dente; drain. Let stand to cool.

Whisk the olive oil, vinegar, lemon juice and mustard in a large serving bowl. Season with salt and pepper. Add the orzo, red tomatoes, yellow tomatoes, feta cheese, pine nuts and basil and toss to mix. Season with additional salt and pepper if desired. Chill, covered, until serving time to allow the flavors to marry. Garnish with sprigs of basil and whole cherry tomatoes.

Veggie Lasagna

SERVES 6 TO 8

16 ounces ricotta cheese
4 cups shredded Italian four-cheese
  blend, divided
2 eggs
4 teaspoons herbes de Provence,
  divided
Salt and black pepper to taste

4 tablespoons extra-virgin olive oil,
  divided
1 medium yellow onion, finely
  chopped
2 red bell peppers, finely chopped
1 yellow bell pepper, finely chopped
1 orange bell pepper, finely chopped

1 bunch kale, stemmed and shredded
  (about 3 cups)
2 cloves garlic, minced
2 (24-ounce) jars tomato basil
  spaghetti sauce
1 (9-ounce) package no-boil lasagna
  noodles

Preheat the oven to 375 degrees.

Combine the ricotta cheese, 2 cups of the Italian cheese, eggs, 2 teaspoons of the herbes de Provence, salt and pepper in a bowl and mix well.

Heat 3 tablespoons of the olive oil in a large sauté pan over medium-high heat. Sauté the onion in the oil for 3 minutes. Add the red peppers, yellow pepper, orange pepper and 1/8 teaspoon salt. Sauté for 10 to 12 minutes or until the vegetables are tender. Add the remaining 1 tablespoon olive oil, kale and garlic. Sauté until the kale is wilted. Season with salt and pepper. Remove from the heat.

Spread about 1 cup of the spaghetti sauce over the bottom of a 9×13-inch baking dish. Add a single layer of the lasagna noodles. Spread with a thin layer of the ricotta mixture and kale mixture. Repeat layers of spaghetti sauce, lasagna noodles, ricotta mixture and kale mixture until all of the ingredients are used, ending with the spaghetti sauce. Sprinkle with the remaining 2 cups Italian cheese and remaining 2 teaspoons herbes de Provence.

Spray a sheet of foil with nonstick cooking spray and cover the lasagna with the foil. Bake the lasagna for 30 minutes. Bake, uncovered, for 15 minutes longer or until the noodles are tender and the cheese is melted. Garnish with chopped fresh basil and parsley.

Main Dishes

Menu
Game Day

Reggie Rivers' Football Sunday Salmon Salad ~ 20

Game Day Dip ~ 41

Asian Marinated Chicken Wings ~ 28

Chili Lime Popcorn ~ 46

Slow-Burn Caramel Popcorn ~ 47

JaMocha Caramel Popcorn ~ 47

Texas-Style Beef Brisket ~ 151

Grilled Corn with Cotija and Lime ~ 215

Irish Stout Chocolate Chunk Cookies ~ 276

Salted Caramel Bars ~ 284

The Power of Play

Kids Connect, a program designed and implemented by the Junior League of Denver, educates and nurtures families with children by focusing on early childhood brain development. JLD volunteers work throughout the year at a Kids Connect curriculum site, educating children and their parents in an interactive play–based environment. The program incorporates reading, art, and music activities. Kids Connect encourages parents to read with their children at home and helps them recognize "teaching moments" in real-life situations.

Forty Garlic Chicken

SERVES 6

2 to 3 pounds boneless chicken
   thighs
¼ cup chopped fresh rosemary
Salt and pepper to taste
1 cup all-purpose flour
3 tablespoons avocado oil

2 tablespoons butter
40 cloves garlic (about 3 heads)
1 cup Champagne or dry white wine
4 cups chicken stock
½ cup heavy cream

Season the chicken with the rosemary, salt and pepper. Coat with the flour. Heat the avocado oil and butter in a large deep skillet over medium-high heat. Cook the chicken in the oil mixture for 3 to 5 minutes per side or until golden brown. Remove to a plate.

Add the garlic to the skillet drippings. Sauté until light brown. Stir in the Champagne and stock. Add the chicken. Simmer, covered, for 30 minutes. Remove the chicken to a plate; keep warm.

Cook the sauce until reduced by two-thirds. Process the sauce and cream in a blender until puréed. Season with salt and pepper if needed. Serve the sauce over the chicken and mashed potatoes.

Chicken and Pancetta with Kalamata Olives

SERVES 8

10 cloves garlic
¼ cup extra-virgin olive oil, divided
1 tablespoon chopped fresh parsley
1 tablespoon chopped fresh chives
1 tablespoon chopped fresh basil

1 teaspoon chopped fresh
   rosemary
½ teaspoon kosher salt
½ teaspoon crushed red
   pepper flakes

8 medium boneless chicken
   thighs or breasts
8 slices pancetta
¾ cup dry white wine
1 cup kalamata olives

Preheat the oven to 450 degrees.

Toss the garlic in a small amount of the olive oil in a bowl. Spread in a large glass baking dish. Combine the remaining olive oil, parsley, chives, basil, rosemary, salt and red pepper flakes in a shallow dish. Coat each chicken thigh with the olive oil mixture and enclose with a slice of pancetta, arranging over the garlic. Roast for 20 minutes. Drizzle with the wine. Roast for 10 minutes longer. Sprinkle with the olives. Roast for 10 minutes longer or to 165 degrees on a meat thermometer.

Chicken Enchiladas Suizas

Favorite recipe from Colorado Collage chosen by Editor Cathy Hollis

SERVES 8

6 boneless skinless chicken breasts
(about 1½ pounds)
1 tablespoon butter
1 cup chopped onion
1 medium green bell pepper, seeded
and chopped
1 medium red bell pepper, seeded
and chopped

8 ounces Cheddar cheese, grated
1 (4-ounce) can diced green chiles
1 cup green chile salsa
½ cup chopped fresh cilantro
2 to 3 canned chipotle chiles in adobo
sauce, chopped (optional)
4 teaspoons ground cumin

Salt and freshly ground pepper to
taste
12 to 15 (7-inch) flour tortillas
10 ounces Monterey Jack cheese,
grated
1 cup whipping cream
½ cup chicken broth

Cook the chicken in enough boiling water to cover in a saucepan for 15 to 20 minutes or until cooked through; drain. Let stand to cool. Shred the chicken.

Preheat the oven to 350 degrees. Grease a 10×15-inch baking pan or 2 smaller pans.

Melt the butter in a medium skillet over medium heat. Cook the onion, green bell pepper and red bell pepper in the butter for 5 to 8 minutes or until tender. Remove to a large bowl. Add the chicken, Cheddar cheese, green chiles, salsa, cilantro, chipotle chiles, cumin, salt and pepper and mix well. Fill each tortilla with about ⅓ cup of the chicken mixture and roll to enclose, arranging seam side down in the prepared baking pan. Sprinkle with the Monterey Jack cheese. May prepare up to this point and chill, covered, for up to 1 day.

Combine the cream and broth in a bowl and mix well. Pour over the enchiladas. Bake, covered with foil, for 30 minutes. Bake, uncovered, for 10 minutes longer or until heated through. Spoon 1 or 2 enchiladas onto each serving plate. Garnish with avocado, tomato and cilantro.

The home of *Colorado Collage* Editor Cathy Hollis is featured as the backdrop for the beautiful Après Anything celebration in this book.

First published in 1995, *Colorado Collage* is a wonderful, historical collection of more than 500 recipes that are true to Colorado. *Collage* celebrates the rugged individualism and unique, healthful ingredients that epitomize the West.

RED CURRY CHICKEN

Red Curry Chicken

SERVES 4

1 cup long grain white rice
8 thin chicken cutlets
Salt and pepper to taste
2 tablespoons canola oil
2 red bell peppers, cut into slices

¼ cup water
1 (15-ounce) can coconut milk
2 tablespoons red curry paste
¼ cup torn fresh basil leaves

Cook the rice according to the package directions.

Season the chicken with salt and pepper. Heat the canola oil in a skillet over medium-high heat. Cook the chicken in the oil in batches for 2 minutes per side or until golden brown and cooked through. Remove to a cutting board, reserving the skillet drippings. Cut the chicken into bite-size pieces. Add the bell peppers and water to the skillet drippings. Cook for 3 to 4 minutes or just until tender, stirring frequently. Stir in the coconut milk and curry paste. Simmer for 4 minutes. Season with salt and pepper. Add the chicken and mix well. Divide the rice and chicken mixture evenly among 4 serving plates. Sprinkle each with 1 tablespoon of the basil. Garnish each plate with a lime wedge.

Chicken Poblano

SERVES 4

3 medium poblano or Anaheim
    peppers
1¼ pounds boneless chicken breasts,
    cut into thin strips
Salt and pepper to taste

4 tablespoons unsalted butter,
    divided
½ cup sliced yellow onion
2 tablespoons brandy
1 cup whipping cream

Preheat the oven to 250 degrees or Warm.

Core the peppers and cut into ¼ to ½ inch slices, wearing gloves. Season the chicken with salt and pepper. Melt 2 tablespoons of the butter in a large skillet over medium-high heat. Sauté the chicken in the butter until cooked through. Remove to an ovenproof serving dish, reserving the skillet drippings. Place the chicken in the oven.

Add the remaining 2 tablespoons butter to the skillet drippings. Sauté the onion in the butter for 3 minutes. Add the poblano peppers. Cook for 5 to 7 minutes or until the peppers are tender, stirring frequently. Add the brandy and stir to deglaze the skillet. Stir in the cream. Cook over high heat for 2 or 3 minutes or until thickened, stirring constantly. Season with salt and pepper. Spoon over the chicken. Serve immediately.

Chicken Stuffed Peppers

SERVES 4

---

4 boneless skinless chicken breasts
6 ounces light cream cheese,
    softened
8 ounces Colby-Jack cheese,
    shredded, divided
1 (15-ounce) can black beans, drained
1 cup frozen corn, thawed
1 cup canned green enchilada sauce

1 (7-ounce) can chopped mild green
    chiles
2 medium jalapeños, seeded and
    minced
1½ teaspoons ground cumin
½ teaspoon (or more) chili powder
¼ teaspoon garlic salt
6 medium red bell peppers

Cook the chicken in enough boiling salted water to cover in a large stockpot until cooked through; drain. Let stand to cool slightly. Shred the chicken.

Preheat the oven to 350 degrees. Line a rimmed baking sheet with foil.

Combine the chicken, cream cheese, 4 ounces of the Colby-Jack cheese, black beans, corn, enchilada sauce, green chiles, jalapeños, cumin, chili powder and garlic salt in a large bowl and mix well.

Cut the bell peppers into halves, starting on the stem side. Core and seed the peppers. Arrange on the prepared baking sheet. Divide the chicken mixture evenly among the peppers. Sprinkle with the remaining 4 ounces Colby-Jack cheese. Bake for 30 to 35 minutes. Broil for 3 to 5 minutes or until the cheese starts to brown. Let stand to cool slightly. Serve with rice and sour cream if desired.

DISCOVER DENVER

Hundreds of breweries call Colorado home. They, along with breweries from all over the US, are showcased every year in the fall when downtown Denver hosts the Great American Beer Festival.

Mustard Tarragon Chicken Sauté

SERVES 4

4 boneless skinless chicken breasts
Salt and pepper to taste
1 ½ tablespoons unsalted butter
⅓ cup finely chopped shallots
⅓ cup dry vermouth

2 tablespoons whole grain Dijon
    mustard
½ cup whipping cream
2 ½ tablespoons chopped fresh
    tarragon, divided

Sprinkle the chicken with salt and pepper. Melt the butter in a large heavy skillet over medium-high heat. Cook the chicken in the butter for 5 minutes per side or until cooked through. Remove to a platter, reserving the skillet drippings. Tent the chicken with foil to keep warm.

Sauté the shallots in the skillet drippings for 1 minute. Stir in the vermouth and mustard. Bring to a simmer. Add the cream and 1½ tablespoons of the tarragon and mix well. Simmer for 5 minutes or just until thickened, stirring frequently. Return the chicken and any accumulated drippings to the skillet. Simmer until the chicken is heated through. Remove the chicken to a platter. Spoon the sauce over the chicken. Sprinkle with the remaining 1 tablespoon tarragon. Serve immediately.

Salsa Grilled Chicken

SERVES 8

1 ⅓ cups salsa or picante sauce
⅔ cup Dijon mustard
2 tablespoons lemon juice

6 tablespoons unsalted butter,
    softened
8 boneless skinless chicken breasts

Combine the salsa, mustard and lemon juice in a bowl and mix well. Reserve ½ cup for basting. Remove 2 tablespoons of the remaining mixture to a mixing bowl. Add the butter and beat until well blended. Shape into a log on waxed paper. Wrap with the waxed paper and chill until serving time.

Arrange the chicken in a large shallow glass dish. Spoon the remaining salsa mixture evenly over the chicken, coating completely. Chill, covered, for 1 to 4 hours.

Preheat the grill to medium.

Grill the chicken for 4 to 5 minutes per side or until cooked through, turning once and basting with the reserved salsa mixture after turning. Remove to each of 8 serving plates. Cut the butter mixture into slices. Place a slice on each chicken breast. Serve immediately.

Spicy Chicken Thighs

SERVES 4

1 tablespoon brown sugar
1 tablespoon ground cumin
1 tablespoon salt
1 tablespoon black pepper
¼ teaspoon cayenne pepper
8 ounces fennel bulbs, cored and cut
   into wedges

8 ounces butternut squash, cut into
   bite-size pieces
1 cup grapes
1 tablespoon extra-virgin olive oil
8 bone-in skin-on chicken thighs
¼ cup fresh cilantro leaves (optional)

Preheat the oven to 425 degrees.

Combine the brown sugar, cumin, salt, black pepper and cayenne pepper in a bowl and mix well. Toss the fennel, squash and grapes in the olive oil in a bowl. Add half of the brown sugar mixture and toss to coat. Spread in a single layer on a rimmed baking sheet.

Coat the chicken with the remaining half of the brown sugar mixture, arranging skin side up on top of the fennel mixture. Roast for 35 minutes. Divide evenly among 4 serving plates and sprinkle with the cilantro.

Thai Lime Chicken Thighs

SERVES 4 TO 6

8 medium bone-in skin-on
   chicken thighs
1 (13-ounce) can coconut milk
3 to 4 tablespoons Thai green
   curry paste

3 tablespoons fish sauce
Grated zest and juice of
   1 medium lime
1 teaspoon salt

Place the chicken in a large bowl. Mix the coconut milk, curry paste, fish sauce, lime zest, lime juice and salt in a small bowl. Pour over the chicken. Chill, covered, for 8 to 12 hours.

Preheat the oven to 425 degrees. Line a large rimmed baking sheet with foil and place a wire rack on the baking sheet.

Remove the chicken from the marinade and pat with paper towels to remove any excess marinade. Arrange skin side down on the prepared wire rack. Roast for 20 minutes. Turn over the chicken. Roast for 20 minutes longer or until cooked through and golden brown. Sprinkle with additional grated lime zest if desired.

SPICY CHICKEN THIGHS

Pistachio-Crusted Chicken with Mustard Cream Sauce

SERVES 4

1 cup shelled unsalted pistachios
(about 4 ounces)
½ cup panko
2 tablespoons Dijon mustard
2 tablespoons chopped fresh basil
1 tablespoon chopped fresh dill

1 teaspoon chopped fresh rosemary
1 teaspoon salt
¼ teaspoon cayenne pepper
4 boneless skinless chicken breasts
2 tablespoons extra-virgin olive oil
Mustard Cream Sauce (recipe below)

Preheat the oven to 400 degrees.

Process the pistachios in a food processor until finely ground. Blend in the panko. Pour into a shallow dish. Combine the mustard, basil, dill, rosemary, salt and cayenne pepper in a bowl and mix well. Spread over both sides of the chicken. Coat with the pistachio mixture.

Heat the olive oil in a large heavy skillet over medium heat. Cook the chicken in the oil for 2 minutes per side or until golden brown. Remove to a baking sheet. Bake for 15 minutes or until cooked through. Spoon the Mustard Cream Sauce over each serving. Serve immediately.

MUSTARD CREAM SAUCE

¼ cup dry white wine
2 tablespoons chopped shallots
½ cup whipping cream
1 tablespoon Dijon mustard

1½ teaspoons chopped fresh basil
1½ teaspoons chopped fresh dill
Salt and pepper to taste

Combine the wine and shallots in a heavy saucepan. Bring to a boil. Boil for 4 minutes or until the liquid has evaporated. Reduce the heat to medium. Add the whipping cream. Simmer for 2 minutes or until reduced by half, stirring occasionally. Stir in the mustard, basil and dill. Simmer for 2 minutes, stirring occasionally. Season with salt and pepper.

Smoked Turkey

SERVES 8 TO 12

Hickory chips
2 to 3 cups extra-virgin olive oil
12 to 20 cloves garlic, peeled
4 to 5 tablespoons cracked black pepper
1 (16-pound) turkey
2 tablespoons kosher salt
1 medium onion, chopped
2 medium green chiles, roasted, or 1 small can chiles
2 ribs celery, coarsely chopped

Soak the hickory chips in water for 24 hours. Combine the olive oil, garlic and pepper in a bowl and mix well. Let stand, covered, for 24 hours.

Place the prepared hickory chips in the smoker or grill.

Make 8 small cups out of foil. Remove the garlic from the olive oil mixture to the foil cups using a slotted spoon, reserving the olive oil mixture. Arrange the cups of garlic in the smoker or on the grill; the garlic will flavor the turkey as it cooks.

Preheat the smoker or grill according to the manufacturer's directions.

Empty the cavity of the turkey. Sprinkle salt over the turkey. Stuff half full with the onion, chiles and celery.

Place a large pan of water with a rack in the smoker or on the grill. Place the turkey on the rack. Smoke or grill for 3 to 4 hours or until the turkey is cooked through, basting occasionally with the reserved olive oil mixture.

Southwest Autumn Acorn Squash

SERVES 6

3 (¾- to 1-pound) acorn squash
10 ounces bulk turkey sausage
1 small onion, chopped
½ medium red bell pepper, chopped
2 cloves garlic, minced
1 tablespoon chili powder
1 teaspoon ground cumin
2 cups grape tomatoes or cherry tomatoes, cut into halves
1 (15-ounce) can black beans, rinsed and drained
½ teaspoon salt
¼ teaspoon (or more) hot sauce
1¼ cups shredded Cheddar cheese

Preheat the oven to 375 degrees. Spray a large baking dish with nonstick cooking spray.

Cut the squash into halves and scoop out the seeds. Arrange cut sides down in the prepared baking dish. Bake for 45 minutes or until tender. Reduce the oven temperature to 325 degrees. Turn over the squash.

Brown the turkey sausage in a skillet over medium heat, stirring to crumble. Add the onion and bell pepper. Cook until tender, stirring frequently. Stir in the garlic, chili powder and cumin. Cook for 30 seconds. Stir in the tomatoes, black beans, salt and hot sauce. Simmer, covered, over medium-low heat for 10 minutes or until the tomatoes have broken down. Divide the mixture evenly among the squash halves. Sprinkle with the Cheddar cheese. Bake for 12 minutes or until heated through and the cheese is melted.

Lemon Garlic Cornish Game Hens

SERVES 2

2 Cornish game hens
2 tablespoons extra-virgin olive oil
1 large lemon, cut into 8 pieces
6 cloves garlic, coarsely chopped

2 tablespoons chopped fresh
    rosemary
1 teaspoon kosher salt
1 teaspoon ground black pepper

Preheat the oven to 450 degrees. Line a roasting pan with foil. Place a rack in the roasting pan and spray with nonstick cooking spray.

Coat the game hens with the olive oil and stuff the cavity with the lemon. Mix the garlic and rosemary in a small bowl. Place a small amount of the mixture under the skin of the breasts of each game hen. Spoon half the remaining mixture into the cavity of each game hen. Tuck the wing tips under the hen. Sprinkle the hens with the salt and pepper. Place the hens on the prepared rack. Roast for 15 minutes. Reduce the oven temperature to 350 degrees. Roast for 40 to 45 minutes longer or to 160 degrees on a meat thermometer, rotating the pan every 15 minutes. Let stand to rest for 10 to 15 minutes before serving. Serve with steamed asparagus and roasted potatoes.

Braciola

SERVES 6 TO 8

6 (¼-inch-thick) top sirloin steaks
    (about 2 pounds)
2 ounces salami, chopped
⅓ cup bread crumbs
⅓ cup chopped fresh parsley
⅓ cup grated Romano cheese
3 tablespoons pine nuts, chopped

4 cloves garlic, finely chopped,
    divided
½ teaspoon salt plus more to taste
½ teaspoon black pepper plus
    more to taste
1 (28-ounce) can Italian crushed
    tomatoes

1 medium yellow onion, finely
    chopped
6 tablespoons olive oil, divided
½ teaspoon red pepper flakes
¼ to ⅓ cup chopped fresh basil

Pound the steaks between plastic wrap using a meat mallet. Combine the salami, bread crumbs, parsley, Romano cheese, pine nuts, 3 cloves of the garlic, ½ teaspoon salt and ½ teaspoon pepper in a bowl and mix well. Divide the mixture evenly among the steaks. Roll to enclose the filling, securing with kitchen string. Season the steaks with salt and pepper to taste.

Combine the tomatoes, onion, 2 tablespoons of the olive oil, remaining garlic clove and red pepper flakes in a large saucepan. Cook over medium heat until heated through, stirring occasionally and adding the basil near the end of the cooking time. Keep warm.

Heat the remaining 4 tablespoons olive oil in a large pan. Brown the steak rolls in the oil for 4 to 6 minutes per side. Remove to the tomato mixture. Simmer, covered, for 1½ to 1¾ hours, stirring frequently.

Prime Rib to Perfection

SERVES 16

1 (8-pound or smaller) prime rib roast
½ cup butter
2 tablespoons herbes de Provence
2 tablespoons black pepper
1½ tablespoons kosher salt
8 to 10 cloves garlic

1 medium onion, chopped
2 medium carrots, chopped
2 ribs celery, chopped
2 cups beef stock
Horseradish Sauce (recipe below)

Bring the roast to room temperature.

Preheat the oven to 500 degrees.

Combine the butter, herbes de Provence and pepper in a bowl and mix well. Spread evenly over the fatty side of the roast. Season all over with the salt. Slit the roast in 8 to 10 places and insert a garlic clove into each slit. Place the roast on a roasting pan and cover with foil.

Bake for 40 minutes for an 8-pound roast or multiply the exact weight of the roast by 5 and cook for that many minutes. Turn off the oven; do not open the oven door. Let the roast stand in the closed oven for 2 hours; roast will be medium-rare. Remove to a cutting board, reserving 1 cup of the pan drippings in the pan.

Place the roasting pan over 2 burners on the stove. Add the onion, carrots and celery. Cook over high heat until browned. Add 1 cup of the stock, stirring constantly. Cook for 2 minutes. Remove to a saucepan. Stir in the remaining 1 cup stock. Simmer for 20 minutes. Season with additional salt and pepper. Pour through a mesh strainer into a bowl; skim off any fat. Slice the roast. Serve the jus and Horseradish Sauce with the roast.

HORSERADISH SAUCE

1 cup sour cream or Greek yogurt
6 tablespoons chopped fresh chives
¼ cup freshly grated horseradish
1 tablespoon Dijon mustard

2 teaspoons lemon juice
1 teaspoon Champagne vinegar
½ teaspoon salt, or to taste
½ teaspoon pepper, or to taste

Whisk the sour cream, chives, horseradish, mustard, lemon juice, vinegar, salt and pepper in a small bowl until blended. Chill, covered, until serving time.

Texas-Style Beef Brisket

SERVES 12

12 pounds full packer prime
   beef brisket
2 tablespoons kosher salt
2 teaspoons dry mustard

2 teaspoons garlic powder
2 teaspoons ancho chile powder
1 teaspoon cayenne pepper
1 cup beef broth

Trim the fat cap of the brisket to ¼ inch or less. Combine the salt, dry mustard, garlic powder, chile powder and cayenne pepper in a small bowl and mix well. Coat the brisket generously with the mixture, doubling the rub if necessary to cover the brisket. Place in a large dish. Chill, covered, for 8 to 12 hours.

Preheat a grill or smoker to 225 degrees.

Grill or smoke the brisket fat side down over indirect heat to 150 to 160 degrees on a meat thermometer. Remove to 2 large layers of heavy-duty foil. Pour the broth carefully over the brisket and wrap tightly with the foil. Return to the grill. Grill over indirect heat to 200 to 205 degrees on a meat thermometer. Wrap the brisket with towels and place in a well-insulated container. Let stand to rest for 1 to 4 hours. Remove the brisket to a cutting board and cut against the grain.

Note: *Since transition points are by temperature, this recipe also works great for a smaller point or flat-cut brisket. Use as much of the rub as needed to coat the brisket well. Store any remaining rub in an airtight container.*

Entertaining Tip

Clean that dirt out of your wheelbarrow, flowerpot, bucket, or barrel and use it as an interesting drink cooler. All you need is plenty of ice and brightly colored bottles to make a fun and functional display.

Roast Beef Tenderloins with Shallot Confit and Wine Sauce

SERVES 6 TO 8

4 tablespoons vegetable oil, divided
4 ounces shiitake mushrooms
   including stems, coarsely chopped
1 small onion, coarsely chopped
1 small carrot, coarsely chopped
1 small rib celery, coarsely chopped

3 cloves garlic, coarsely chopped
2 fresh sage leaves
1 sprig of fresh rosemary
1 sprig of fresh thyme
1½ cups dry red wine
½ cup ruby red port

4 cups beef stock or broth
2 (2-pound) beef tenderloins
   (preferably center cut)
Salt and pepper to taste
Shallot Confit (recipe below)
2 tablespoons unsalted butter

Heat 2 tablespoons of the vegetable oil in a large saucepan. Add the mushrooms, onion, carrot, celery, garlic, sage, rosemary and thyme. Cook over medium heat for 12 minutes or until the vegetables begin to brown, stirring frequently. Add the wine and port. Cook over high heat for 10 minutes or until reduced to ¼ cup, stirring occasionally. Add the stock. Simmer over medium-low heat until reduced to 2 cups, stirring occasionally. Strain the mixture into a saucepan, pressing the solids to extract as much liquid as possible; discard the solids.

Preheat the oven to 400 degrees.

Heat the remaining 2 tablespoons vegetable oil in a large ovenproof skillet. Season the tenderloins with salt and pepper. Cook the tenderloins in the oil for 12 minutes, turning to brown all sides, ending with the smooth side up. Spread with the Shallot Confit. Roast for 30 minutes or to 125 degrees for rare. Remove to a cutting board, reserving the drippings in the skillet. Let the tenderloins stand to rest, covered with foil, for 10 minutes.

Cook the skillet drippings over high heat until the mixture sizzles. Whisk in the wine mixture. Simmer for 3 minutes, stirring occasionally. Remove from the heat. Add the butter 1 tablespoon at a time, whisking until blended after each addition. Season with salt and pepper. Pour into a gravy boat. Serve the tenderloins with the wine sauce.

SHALLOT CONFIT

8 ounces shallots, cut into
   ¼-inch slices
1 cup dry red wine

½ cup ruby red port
1 sprig of fresh thyme
1 teaspoon sugar

Preheat the oven to 350 degrees. Combine the shallots, wine, port, thyme and sugar in a small shallow baking dish. Bake, covered with foil, for 1 hour. Bake, uncovered, for 30 minutes or until the shallots are tender and most of the liquid has evaporated. Discard the thyme.

Flank Steak with Chimichurri

SERVES 4 TO 6

1½ pounds trimmed flank steak
2 teaspoons ground cumin
1½ teaspoons kosher salt, divided
1 teaspoon ground coriander

¼ teaspoon black pepper
3 large cloves garlic
1 cup packed fresh cilantro
1 cup packed fresh Italian parsley

¼ cup (or more) white vinegar
⅓ cup (or more) extra-virgin olive oil
⅛ teaspoon cayenne pepper or red
    pepper flakes

Preheat the broiler or grill to medium.

Pat the steak dry with paper towels. Combine the cumin, 1 teaspoon of the salt, coriander and black pepper in a small bowl and mix well. Rub over both sides of the steak. Grill the steak or broil 3 inches from the heat source for 5 to 7 minutes per side for medium-rare. Remove to a cutting board. Let stand to rest for 5 minutes or longer.

Process the garlic in a food processor just until chopped. Add the cilantro, parsley, vinegar, olive oil, remaining ½ teaspoon salt and cayenne pepper. Process until the herbs are finely chopped, adding additional vinegar and/or olive oil if needed for the desired consistency. Cut the steak against the grain. Serve with the chimichurri.

Marinated Flank Steak

SERVES 4 TO 6

¼ cup coconut aminos or tamari
½ cup extra-virgin olive oil
¼ cup rice vinegar
2 tablespoons minced ginger root

2 teaspoons Worcestershire sauce
1 teaspoon minced garlic
1½ pounds flank steak

Combine the coconut aminos, olive oil, vinegar, ginger, Worcestershire sauce and garlic in a large sealable plastic bag. Add the steak and turn to coat. Chill for 8 to 12 hours.

Let the steak stand at room temperature for 15 to 30 minutes.

Preheat the grill to medium-high or 400 to 425 degrees.

Grill the steak, covered, for 5 minutes. Turn over the steak. Grill for 4 to 5 minutes or until done to taste. Remove to a cutting board. Let stand to rest for 10 minutes. Cut against the grain into thin diagonal slices. Serve immediately.

Veal Osso Buco

SERVES 6

6 veal shanks (12 to 16 ounces each)
Salt and pepper to taste
4 to 5 tablespoons all-purpose flour,
    divided
½ cup vegetable oil
2 medium red onions, chopped

2 carrots, chopped
2 ribs celery, chopped
2 cloves garlic, minced
1 tablespoon tomato paste
⅛ teaspoon saffron threads

½ bottle dry white wine
    (about 1½ cups)
2 bay leaves
3 cups chicken stock, heated
4 cups beef stock, heated

Preheat the oven to 300 degrees.

Pat the veal shanks dry with paper towels. Season with salt and pepper and coat with 3 to 4 tablespoons of the flour. Heat the vegetable oil in a large heavy casserole pot or Dutch oven. Brown the veal on all sides in the oil. Remove to a plate.

Sauté the onions, carrots, celery and garlic in the drippings in the pot until tender. Stir in the remaining 1 tablespoon flour, tomato paste and saffron. Cook for 2 to 3 minutes, stirring frequently. Stir in the wine and bay leaves. Return the veal to the pot. Add the chicken stock and beef stock.

Bake, covered, for 4 hours. Remove the veal to a plate, reserving the drippings in the pot. Season the drippings with salt and pepper. Cook over high heat until reduced to the desired consistency; discard the bay leaves. Serve the veal with the sauce and mashed potatoes or polenta.

Entertaining Tip

Select serving dishes and utensils before you start cooking. Use notes to mark what menu item will go in each dish. You won't be scrambling to find dishes as you're putting food on the table, and you'll know you have enough space on your buffet or table for all the food.

Seasoned Hamburgers

SERVES 4 TO 6

1 cup light soy sauce
1 medium onion
3 or 4 cloves garlic
2 tablespoons Beau Monde seasoning

2 tablespoons Gravy Master® or
   Kitchen Bouquet®
1 to 1½ pounds ground beef

Process the soy sauce, onion, garlic and Beau Monde seasoning in a food processor until blended. Add the Gravy Master and pulse to blend. Combine the ground beef and marinade in a bowl and mix gently to incorporate; the ground beef should be wet but not runny. Shape into 4 to 6 patties.

Preheat the grill to high.

Grill the burgers for 3 minutes or until golden brown on the bottom. Turn over the burgers. Grill for 4 to 5 minutes or to desired temperature.

Jalapeño Meat Loaf

SERVES 6

1½ tablespoons butter
1 medium yellow onion
½ cup minced bell pepper
   (any color)
½ teaspoon ground jalapeño
½ teaspoon cayenne pepper

½ teaspoon (or more) onion
   powder, divided
½ teaspoon garlic powder
   Salt and pepper to taste
¾ to 1 pound ground beef

¼ to ⅓ pound ground pork
1 egg, beaten
¼ cup ketchup
¼ cup bread crumbs
¼ to ⅓ cup grated Parmesan cheese

Preheat the oven to 350 degrees.

Melt the butter in a small nonstick skillet. Add the onion, bell pepper, ground jalapeño, cayenne pepper, ½ teaspoon of the onion powder and garlic powder. Season generously with salt and pepper. Sauté until the onion is translucent. Let stand to cool.

Place the ground beef and ground pork in a large bowl. Season with salt, pepper and additional onion powder and mix well. Add the onion mixture and mix well. Stir in the egg and ketchup. Add the bread crumbs and Parmesan cheese and mix well. Shape into a 1½- to 2-inch-thick loaf in a glass baking dish. Bake for 75 to 90 minutes or until well browned.

Italian Meatballs

SERVES 8

3 cups Italian bread crumbs
1½ cups milk
1 pound ground sirloin
1 pound ground pork
1 pound ground veal

3 large eggs , beaten
1 cup grated Parmesan cheese
1 bunch fresh basil or parsley,
    chopped
Salt and pepper to taste

Preheat the oven to 350 degrees. Grease a baking pan generously.

Combine the bread crumbs and milk in a large bowl. Let stand until most of the milk is absorbed. Add the ground sirloin, ground pork, ground veal, eggs, Parmesan cheese, basil, salt and pepper and mix gently, adding warm water if mixture is too thick. Shape into balls, arranging in the prepared baking pan. Bake for 45 minutes, watching carefully and turning halfway through the baking time. Broil for 2 minutes or until browned.

Colorado Lamb Meatballs

SERVES 4 TO 6

1 pound ground lamb
1 cup shredded sharp Cheddar
    cheese
1 cup finely chopped fresh parsley
3 slices soft bread, cut into ⅜-inch
    cubes (about 1 cup)

⅓ cup finely chopped onion
2 cloves garlic, minced
1 egg, lightly beaten
1 teaspoon lemon pepper
½ teaspoon salt
½ teaspoon black pepper

2 tablespoons butter
1 (15-ounce) can tomato sauce
⅓ cup (or more) grated Parmesan
    cheese

Preheat the oven to 375 degrees.

Combine the ground lamb, Cheddar cheese, parsley, bread, onion, garlic, egg, lemon pepper, salt and black pepper in a bowl and mix gently. Shape into 1½- to 2-inch balls. Brown the meatballs in the butter in a skillet over medium-low heat, turning frequently and working in batches if needed. Remove to a baking dish.

Pour the tomato sauce over the meatballs. Sprinkle with the Parmesan cheese. Bake, covered, for 20 minutes. Bake, uncovered, for an additional 10 minutes. Serve with wide egg noodles or baked spaghetti squash.

Roast Leg of Lamb

SERVES 6 TO 8

1 cup extra-virgin olive oil
¼ cup balsamic vinegar
¼ cup honey
1 tablespoon coarsely ground
   black pepper

1 tablespoon red pepper flakes
1 fresh bay leaf, chopped
Leaves of 4 sprigs of fresh thyme
2 tablespoons minced fresh
   rosemary leaves

2 tablespoons minced fresh mint
6 pounds semi-boneless leg of lamb
Kosher salt to taste
Tapenade (recipe below)

Whisk the olive oil, vinegar, honey, pepper, red pepper flakes, bay leaf, thyme, rosemary and mint in a bowl until blended.

Preheat the oven to 400 degrees.

Coat the lamb with the olive oil mixture and season with salt. Place on a rack in a roasting pan. Roast for 20 minutes. Reduce the oven temperature to 325 degrees. Roast for 1½ to 1¾ hours longer or until a meat thermometer inserted into the thickest portion registers 130 to 135 degrees for medium-rare. Cover the lamb loosely with foil. Let stand to rest for 30 minutes. Remove to a cutting board and carve. Serve with the Tapenade.

TAPENADE

1 cup kalamata olives, pitted
¼ cup drained capers
2 cloves garlic
2 anchovy fillets

2 tablespoons chopped fresh basil
2 tablespoons chopped fresh
   Italian parsley
2 tablespoons chopped fresh oregano

½ to 1 cup extra-virgin olive oil
1 tablespoon honey, or more to taste
Kosher salt to taste

Combine the kalamata olives, capers, garlic, anchovies, basil, parsley and oregano in a food processor. Add the desired amount of the olive oil in a fine stream, processing constantly. Add the honey and salt and process just until blended. Spoon into a bowl.

Note: *Most butchers will have semi-boneless leg of lamb, which is formed by removing the aitchbone and tying that section of the lamb to make it easier to carve.*

Shepherd's Pie with Mushrooms, Stout and Horseradish Potatoes

The American Lamb Board serves up lamb-spirational recipes, facts, news, and views. They are an industry-funded research and promotions commodity board that represents all sectors of the American Lamb industry. Its work is overseen by the US Department of Agriculture. The board's programs are supported and implemented by Denver-based staff that will teach you everything you need to know about lamb! americanlamb.com

SERVES 6

2 pounds American lamb stew meat, or lamb shoulder or leg, cut into 1-inch cubes

2 ½ teaspoons salt, divided, plus more to taste

Fresh ground pepper to taste

2 tablespoons extra-virgin olive oil

6 tablespoons unsalted butter, divided

1 large yellow onion, chopped

3 medium carrots, peeled and cut into ¼-inch slices

3 ribs celery, cut into ¼-inch slices

8 ounces cremini or button mushrooms, cut into halves

2 medium cloves garlic, minced

6 tablespoons all-purpose flour

2 cups lamb stock or low-sodium beef broth

1 cup Irish stout (such as Guinness)

2 teaspoons fresh rosemary leaves

2 ½ pounds Yukon Gold potatoes, peeled and cut into large pieces

1 cup sour cream

3 tablespoons prepared horseradish

1 cup frozen peas

Preheat the oven to 325 degrees.

Season the lamb with 1½ teaspoons of the salt and pepper to taste. Heat the olive oil in a Dutch oven over medium-high heat. Cook the lamb in the oil for 8 minutes or until browned on all sides, working in batches and stirring occasionally. Remove batches to a plate, reserving the drippings in the pan.

Add 2 tablespoons of the butter to the drippings in the Dutch oven. Cook over medium heat until the butter is melted. Add the onion, carrots, celery, mushrooms and garlic. Cook, covered, for 5 minutes or just until the vegetables are tender, stirring occasionally. Sprinkle with the flour and stir to mix. Add the stock 1 cup at a time, stirring to mix completely after each addition. Stir in the stout, rosemary and remaining 1 teaspoon salt. Bring to a boil over medium-high heat, stirring occasionally. Return the lamb to the Dutch oven. Bake, covered, for 1½ hours or until the lamb is tender.

Combine the potatoes and enough water to cover by 1 inch in a large saucepan. Season generously with additional salt; cover. Bring to a boil over high heat. Simmer, uncovered, over medium heat for 20 to 25 minutes or until tender; drain and return to the saucepan. Cut 3 tablespoons of the butter into cubes. Add to the potatoes. Mash the potatoes, adding the sour cream gradually. Stir in the horseradish. Season with additional salt.

Remove the stew from the oven. Adjust the seasonings. Stir in the peas. Increase the oven temperature to 400 degrees.

Spoon the stew into a 3-quart baking dish. Spread evenly with the mashed potatoes, using a fork to make decorative lines or peaks. Cut the remaining 1 tablespoon butter into cubes. Dot the top of the potatoes with the butter. Bake for 20 to 30 minutes or until the potatoes are crusty and browned in places. Let stand for 5 minutes before serving.

Pork Tenderloin with Banana Chutney

SERVES 6

1 (1½-pound) pork tenderloin
1 teaspoon salt plus more to taste
Pepper to taste
2 teaspoons ground cumin
1 tablespoon extra-virgin olive oil

3 bananas, chopped
⅓ cup apple cider vinegar,
   or more sto taste
¾ cup sugar
⅓ cup raisins

3 whole cloves
¼ teaspoon ground cinnamon
¼ teaspoon cayenne pepper

Preheat the oven to 400 degrees.

Rub the tenderloin with salt to taste and pepper to taste and sprinkle with the cumin. Heat the olive oil in a large ovenproof skillet over medium-high heat. Cook the tenderloin for 2 minutes per side or until browned. Bake for 20 to 30 minutes or to 145 degrees on a meat thermometer. Remove to a cutting board. Let stand to rest for 5 minutes.

Meanwhile, combine the bananas and vinegar in a heavy saucepan. Cook over medium heat for 5 to 7 minutes or until pulpy. Remove from the heat. Add the sugar, raisins, remaining 1 teaspoon salt, cloves, cinnamon and cayenne pepper and stir until the sugar is dissolved. Let stand for 10 to 15 minutes. Remove and discard the cloves.

Cut the tenderloin against the grain into 1-inch-thick slices, arranging on each of 6 plates. Spoon equal portions of the banana chutney over each serving.

DISCOVER DENVER

Denver is proud to host an array of professional sports teams—from football and baseball, to hockey and basketball, to soccer, lacrosse, and rugby—entertaining crowds all year long. It all started in 1960 when the Broncos became the first major league team to arrive. The historic home of the Broncos, Mile High Stadium was demolished in 2002 to make room for a new modern field right next door. Every fall, Denver turns orange and blue as "Broncomania" takes hold of the Mile High City.

Winter Pork Roast with Port Sauce

SERVES 8

4 ounces dried apricots, cut into
   ½-inch pieces
¼ cup pitted prunes, cut into
   ½-inch pieces
⅔ cup ruby port
1 medium onion, finely chopped

1 small shallot, finely chopped
6 tablespoons unsalted butter
1 tart apple (such as Granny Smith),
   peeled, cored and cut into
   ½-inch slices
2 teaspoons salt, divided

1 teaspoon pepper, divided
1 (6-pound) pork loin roast with 10 ribs,
   frenched, at room temperature
9 or 10 slices bacon
Port Sauce (recipe below)

Combine the apricots, prunes and port in a small heavy saucepan. Simmer, covered, for 5 minutes. Let stand for 10 minutes.

Cook the onion and shallot in the butter in a 12-inch heavy skillet over medium heat for 4 to 5 minutes or until tender, stirring occasionally. Add the apple, ½ teaspoon of the salt and ½ teaspoon of the pepper. Cook for 5 minutes or until the apple is tender, stirring occasionally. Stir in the apricot mixture. Let stand to cool.

Preheat the oven to 500 degrees, moving the oven rack to the center position.

Cut a 1½-inch-wide horizontal slit though the center of the pork using a long thin knife and working from both ends, creating a pocket. Cut a vertical slit at the center of the pork to widen the pocket, cutting to the horizontal slit. Stuff the pocket with the apricot mixture using the handle of a wooden spoon, working from both sides if needed and reserving the remaining apricot mixture for the Port Sauce.

Season the pork with the remaining 1½ teaspoons salt and ½ teaspoon pepper. Place in a large heavy roasting pan. Place a slice of bacon between each rib bone, tucking the ends under the pork. Roast for 20 minutes. Reduce the oven temperature to 325 degrees. Roast the pork for 1½ to 1¾ hours or until a meat thermometer inserted 2 inches into the center of the roast registers 155 degrees. Remove to a cutting board, reserving the drippings in the pan for the Port Sauce. Cover the pork loosely with foil. Let stand to rest for 15 to 20 minutes or to 160 degrees on the meat thermometer; the pork will be slightly pink. Cut the roast between the ribs into chops. Serve the stuffed chops with the Port Sauce.

PORT SAUCE

Reserved pan drippings
½ cup ruby port
1 small shallot, finely chopped

1½ cups low-sodium chicken
   stock, divided
Reserved apricot mixture

1 teaspoon arrowroot or cornstarch
Salt and pepper to taste

Skim the fat from the reserved pan drippings, reserving 1½ tablespoons fat. Place the roasting pan with the remaining pan drippings over 2 burners over high heat. Add the port. Cook for 1 minute, stirring constantly and scraping up any brown bits from the bottom of the pan. Strain through a mesh strainer into a bowl; discard the solids.

Cook the shallot in the reserved fat in a medium heavy saucepan over medium heat for 3 minutes or until tender, stirring occasionally. Stir in the pan drippings, 1¼ cups of the stock and reserved apricot mixture. Bring to a simmer. Whisk the

arrowroot and remaining ¼ cup stock in a small bowl until smooth. Add the arrowroot mixture and any juices from the cutting board to the stock mixture. Simmer for 5 minutes or just until thickened, whisking occasionally. Season with salt and pepper.

Note: *The stuffing may be made 2 days ahead and stored in a covered container in the refrigerator. The flavor of the pork will be better if stuffed, seasoned and wrapped with bacon 1 day ahead and chilled. Bring to room temperature before roasting.*

Sweet and Spicy Pork

SERVES 4

2 to 4 tablespoons extra-virgin olive oil or sesame oil
½ large sweet onion, cut into large pieces
2 poblano peppers, cut into large pieces
⅓ large yellow bell pepper, cut into large pieces

⅓ large red bell pepper, cut into large pieces
1 small cabbage, cut into large pieces
½ teaspoon garlic powder, divided
½ teaspoon onion powder, divided
¼ teaspoon white pepper, divided
Salt and black pepper to taste

3 thick-cut boneless pork chops, cut into 4 or 5 strips each
Soy sauce to taste
2 very firm nectarines with peel, cut into thick slices
1½ cups broccoli florets
1½ cups cauliflower florets
½ can cola or diet cola

Heat a large skillet or pan over medium-high heat for 4 to 5 minutes. Add 2 tablespoons olive oil and heat for 20 seconds. Sauté the onion, poblano peppers, yellow pepper, red pepper and cabbage in the oil until the onions are translucent, seasoning with a third each of the garlic powder, onion powder and white pepper. Season with salt and black pepper. Remove the vegetables to a bowl using a slotted spoon; reserve.

Brown the pork on both sides in the skillet drippings, adding more of the olive oil if needed and seasoning with half each of the remaining garlic powder, onion powder and white pepper. Season with salt and black pepper. Stir in soy sauce. Remove the pork to a bowl using a slotted spoon.

Add the nectarines, broccoli and cauliflower to the skillet drippings. Season with the remaining garlic powder, remaining onion powder and remaining white pepper. Season with salt and black pepper. Stir in soy sauce and cola. Return the reserved vegetables to the skillet. Cook until the cauliflower is done to taste. Add the pork and cook just until heated through. Serve with rice.

Thai Pork Ribs

SERVES 4

2 bunches scallions, trimmed
1 (3-inch) fresh ginger root, sliced, or
  equivalent ginger paste
8 large cloves garlic
1 bunch fresh cilantro with stems
6 tablespoons soy sauce

2 tablespoons fish sauce
2 tablespoons sugar
1 teaspoon kosher salt
1 teaspoon coarsely ground
  black pepper
2 to 3 pounds pork spare ribs

Combine the scallions, ginger, garlic, cilantro, soy sauce, fish sauce, sugar, salt and pepper in a blender. Process until the mixture is a loose, finely chopped paste.

Place the ribs in a large bowl or sealable plastic bag. Add the scallion mixture and turn to coat. Chill, covered, for 3 to 12 hours.

Preheat the oven to 350 degrees.

Arrange the ribs bone sides down in a baking pan. Pour the marinade over the ribs. Bake, covered, for 1 hour. Bake, uncovered, for 30 to 40 minutes or until very tender and well browned.

DISCOVER DENVER

Located just north of downtown, Denver's River North Art District (RiNo) is an eclectic collection of creative businesses, galleries, studios, breweries, restaurants, and bars. Each year the neighborhood hosts the CRUSH WALLS graffiti and street art festival. Artists from around the world transform RiNo's walls and alleys into a unique outdoor gallery. Mural by Douglas Hoekzema, aka Hoxxoh.

Tangerine-Glazed Ham with Fresh Sage

SERVES 8

1 (8- to 10-pound) bone-in skin-on
   smoked ham
Salt and pepper to taste
Leaves of 1 bunch fresh sage, divided
¼ cup extra-virgin olive oil
1 cup butter
2 tangerines, cut into thin slices

2 cups tangerine juice
2 cups packed light brown sugar
1 cup water
¼ teaspoon whole cloves
2 sticks cinnamon
1½ pounds carrots, peeled

Preheat the oven to 250 degrees.

Place the ham fat side up in a large roasting pan. Score the ham all over ½ inch deep in a diamond pattern. Season with salt and pepper. Chop most of the sage. Combine the chopped sage and olive oil in a bowl and mix well. Rub over the ham, inserting some of the sage into the slits. Bake the ham for 2 hours.

Heat a saucepan briefly over medium heat. Add the butter, tangerines, tangerine juice, brown sugar, water, cloves and cinnamon. Cook for 30 to 40 minutes or until syrupy. Pour over the ham, arranging some of the tangerines on top. Sprinkle with the remaining sage. Bake for 1½ hours, basting every 30 minutes. Add the carrots to the glaze in the pan. Bake for 30 minutes or until the carrots are tender and the ham is browned. Remove the ham to a cutting board. Let rest for a few minutes before carving. Remove the carrots to a serving dish using a slotted spoon. Pour the glaze into a gravy boat. Serve the ham with the carrots and glaze. Garnish with sprigs of fresh sage.

Entertaining Tip

Adding a charger plate to your tablescape elevates the design of the table, giving it a more polished and complete look. For a more casual design, forgo the charger plate and pick a textured napkin folded nicely in the middle of the place setting.

Grilled Seafood Packets

SERVES 8

32 littleneck or cherrystone clams in
    shells (about 2½ pounds)
32 medium shrimp in shells
    (about 1¼ pounds)
32 sea scallops (about 2½ pounds)
8 ears corn, husked and cut
    into fourths

32 large cherry tomatoes
Lemon Butter or Chive Butter
    (recipes below)
Fresh chive stems or chopped fresh
    chives (optional)

Preheat the grill to medium, placing the grill rack 4 to 5 inches from the heat source.

Combine 4 each of the clams, shrimp, scallops, corn quarters and cherry tomatoes on each of 8 layers of 8×12-inch foil and parchment paper. Drizzle with equal portions of the Lemon Butter or Chive Butter. Fold the parchment paper and foil into a packet, making tight ½-inch folds and allowing space on the sides for circulation and expansion.

Grill the packets, covered, for 15 to 20 minutes or until the clams are open, the shrimp are pink and firm and the vegetables are tender. Remove to individual plates. Cut a large × across the top of each packet and fold back the foil. Top with chives.

LEMON BUTTER

½ cup butter, melted
1 tablespoon grated lemon zest

Combine the butter and lemon zest in a bowl and mix well.

CHIVE BUTTER

½ cup butter, melted
1 tablespoon chopped fresh chives

Combine the butter and chives in a bowl and mix well.

Zesty Seared Shrimp

SERVES 5 TO 6

3 tablespoons extra-virgin olive oil, divided
2 pounds extra-jumbo shrimp, peeled and deveined
Kosher salt and ground pepper to taste

¾ teaspoon ground turmeric
¼ teaspoon ground curry
10 cloves garlic, minced
6 scallions, thinly sliced
1½ jalapeños, seeded (optional) and finely diced or sliced

½ teaspoon Spanish smoked paprika
½ cup coarsely chopped fresh cilantro, divided
½ teaspoon honey
¼ cup fresh lime juice

Heat 1 tablespoon of the olive oil in a large skillet over medium-high heat. Pat the shrimp dry with paper towels. Season with salt and pepper. Cook the shrimp in the oil in batches for 2 minutes or just until cooked through, turning once and adding additional oil if needed. Remove to a plate, reserving the drippings in the skillet. Reduce the heat to medium.

Add the remaining 2 tablespoons olive oil to the skillet drippings. Add the turmeric and curry. Cook for 30 seconds, stirring constantly. Add the garlic, scallions, jalapeños and paprika and mix well. Return the shrimp and any drippings on the plate to the skillet. Add half the cilantro and toss to coat well. Drizzle with the honey. Cook for 1 minute or until cooked through. Remove from the heat. Pour the lime juice over the shrimp mixture and toss to coat. Season with additional salt, honey and/or lime juice if needed. Sprinkle with the remaining half of the cilantro. Serve with steaming hot rice.

Entertaining Tip

Lawn games are a great way to get your guests outdoors and out of your kitchen. Get them outside with music and drinks. Keep them there with a few fun activities to play together.

Champagne Shrimp

SERVES 4 TO 6

1 cup Champagne or other sparkling dry wine	24 large to extra-large shrimp, peeled with tails intact, deveined	1 tablespoon minced fresh chives
¼ cup extra-virgin olive oil	Champagne Beurre Blanc (recipe below)	1 tablespoon minced fresh tarragon
3 tablespoons minced shallots		1 tablespoon minced fresh parsley
¼ teaspoon whole black peppercorns		

Combine the Champagne, olive oil, shallots and peppercorns in a sealable plastic bag. Add the shrimp and shake to coat the shrimp evenly. Marinate at room temperature for 30 to 60 minutes, turning the bag occasionally.

Preheat the broiler. Spray a broiler pan with nonstick cooking spray.

Drain the shrimp, discarding the marinade. Arrange the shrimp in a single layer on the prepared pan. Broil for 2 minutes per side or just until the centers are opaque. Spoon the warm Champagne Beurre Blanc around the shrimp on a large serving platter or on individual plates. Sprinkle with a mixture of the chives, tarragon and parsley. Serve immediately.

Note: *For a fun spin on classic shrimp and grits, pair with Cauliflower Grits (recipe page 212). May also be served with bread for dipping.*

CHAMPAGNE BEURRE BLANC

2 cups Champagne or other sparkling dry wine	1 cup cold unsalted butter, cut into 16 pieces
⅓ cup finely chopped shallots	Salt and pepper to taste
2 tablespoons Champagne vinegar or white wine vinegar	

Combine the Champagne, shallots and vinegar in a medium heavy saucepan. Bring to a boil. Boil for 20 minutes or until reduced to ¼ cup. Reduce the heat to medium-low. Add the butter 1 piece at a time, whisking to incorporate after each addition; do not boil. Season with salt and pepper.

Chili Coconut Shrimp with Jasmine Rice

SERVES 4

2 tablespoons extra-virgin olive oil
1 pound large shrimp, peeled and
   deveined
2 cloves garlic, minced
1 teaspoon salt
1 (14-ounce) can coconut milk

2 tablespoons chili paste
4 cups cooked jasmine rice
1 tablespoon fresh lime juice
1 scallion, thinly sliced
¼ cup fresh basil, chopped

Heat the olive oil in a large skillet over medium heat. Add the shrimp, garlic and salt. Cook for 5 minutes or just until the shrimp turn pink and are cooked through. Remove the shrimp to a plate, reserving the drippings in the skillet.

Add the coconut milk and chili paste to the skillet drippings. Bring to a boil. Reduce the heat to medium-low. Simmer for 5 minutes or until reduced by half, stirring occasionally. Add the rice, lime juice, scallion and shrimp. Cook for 3 to 4 minutes or just until heated through. Divide evenly among each of 4 plates. Sprinkle each with equal portions of the basil.

DISCOVER DENVER

The beloved Big Blue Bear has become an iconic symbol of Denver. Standing at forty feet tall, the bear peers into the lobby of the Colorado Convention Center. The work, by deceased local artist Lawrence Argent, is actually titled "I See What You Mean." Installed in 2005, the bear has become a favorite photo op for locals and tourists alike.

Shrimp and Sausage Jambalaya

SERVES 8

2 tablespoons extra-virgin olive oil
1 pound medium shrimp, peeled and
   deveined
1 pound smoked ham, cut into cubes
1 pound andouille sausage,
   cut into slices

2 large cloves garlic, minced
2 large ribs celery, chopped
1 green or red bell pepper, chopped
1 large onion, chopped
1½ cups long grain rice
1 (16-ounce) can diced tomatoes

4 cups chicken broth
1½ tablespoons Worcestershire sauce
1 teaspoon salt
¼ teaspoon cayenne pepper,
   or to taste
½ cup chopped fresh parsley, divided

Heat the olive oil in a large stockpot over high heat. Cook the shrimp in the oil for 3 minutes or just until browned, stirring constantly. Remove the shrimp to a plate using a slotted spoon, reserving the drippings in the stockpot.

Add the ham and sausage to the drippings in the stockpot. Cook for 3 to 5 minutes or until browned. Reduce the heat to medium. Stir in the garlic, celery, bell pepper and onion. Cook for 10 minutes or until the vegetables are tender, stirring frequently. Reduce the heat to low.

Add the rice, tomatoes, broth, Worcestershire sauce, salt, cayenne pepper and ¼ cup of the parsley. Cook, covered, for 20 minutes until the rice is plumped and the liquid is absorbed. Stir in the shrimp and remaining ¼ cup parsley. Cook for 3 to 5 minutes or until heated through. Serve immediately.

Steamed Mussels and Pomme Frites

SERVES 6 TO 8

4 to 5 large cloves garlic, thinly sliced
¼ teaspoon red pepper flakes
4 tablespoons butter
2 tablespoons olive oil
1 (28-ounce) can peeled tomatoes
¾ cup dry white wine
3 tablespoons chopped fresh parsley

¾ teaspoon dried thyme
¾ teaspoon salt
2 pounds fresh or frozen mussels
2 to 3 tablespoons Italian bread
   crumbs
1½ tablespoons fresh lemon juice
Pomme Frites (recipe below)

Sauté the garlic and red pepper flakes in the butter and olive oil in a large lidded saucepan over medium-high heat. Add the tomatoes, mashing with a wooden spoon. Stir in the wine, parsley, thyme and salt. Simmer over low heat for 1 hour. Add the mussels. Cook, covered, over high heat for 3 minutes. Rotate the saucepan in a circular pattern to mix the contents, keeping the lid firmly in place. Remove and discard any unopened mussels. Add the bread crumbs and lemon juice; cover. Rotate the saucepan to mix the contents. Bring to a simmer. Serve with Pomme Frites and crusty Italian bread for dipping in the sauce. Garnish with sprigs of fresh thyme.

POMME FRITES

7 cups duck fat
3 cups canola oil
4 large russet potatoes,
   cut into ¼-inch batons
Salt to taste

Heat the duck fat and canola oil to 325 degrees in a 6-quart Dutch oven over medium-high heat.

Deep-fry the potatoes in batches for 5 to 6 minutes or until pale and tender, turning occasionally and removing to a wire rack placed over a baking sheet using a slotted spoon, reserving the duck fat mixture at room temperature. Chill the fries for 1 hour. Heat the duck fat mixture to 400 degrees over medium-high heat. Deep-fry the fries in batches for 1 to 2 minutes or until golden brown and crisp, turning occasionally and removing to a wire rack placed over a baking sheet using a slotted spoon. Season with salt. Serve immediately.

SEA SCALLOPS

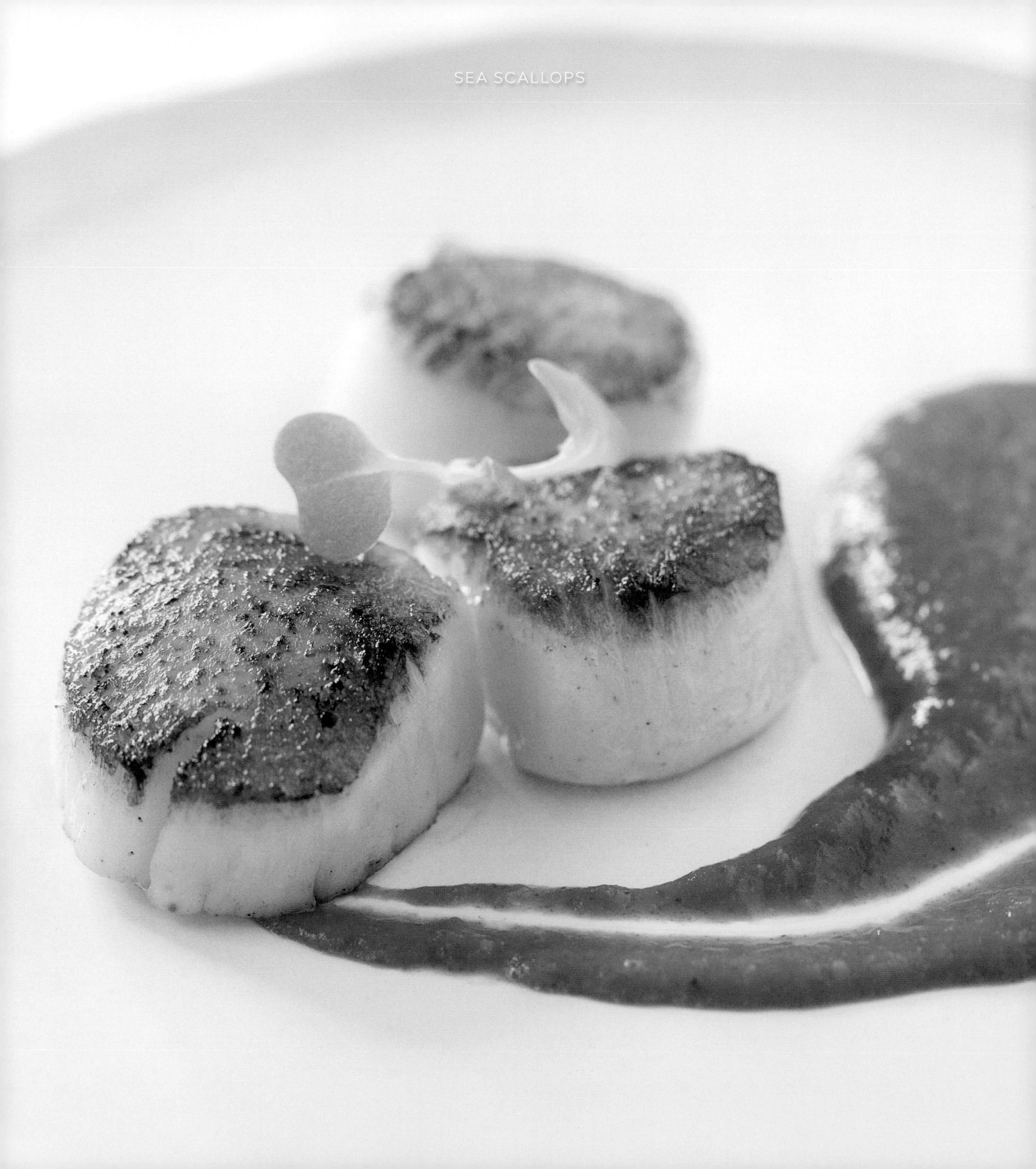

Sea Scallops with Red Pepper Coulis

SERVES 4

3 shallots, finely chopped
2 tablespoons butter, divided
4 medium red bell peppers, peeled
   and julienned, or 4 prepared
   roasted bell peppers, julienned
1½ cups chicken stock

1 tablespoon smoked paprika
Salt and pepper to taste
Vegetable oil
16 sea scallops, cleaned and dried
2 tablespoons butter, melted

Sauté the shallots in 1 tablespoon of the butter in a skillet until tender. Add the bell peppers. Cook until tender. Stir in the stock. Simmer for 10 to 15 minutes or until the liquid is reduced by half. Process in a blender until puréed. Add the remaining 1 tablespoon butter, paprika, salt and pepper and mix well.

Heat the skillet over high heat. Add enough vegetable oil to coat the bottom of the skillet. Season the scallops with salt. Cook in the oil for 3 minutes or until golden brown. Add the melted butter, spooning over the scallops. Turn over the scallops. Cook for 1 minute; do not overcook. Serve immediately with the red pepper coulis and a microgreen garnish.

Halibut with Lemon and Toasted Shallots

SERVES 4

4 tablespoons butter, softened
3 tablespoons lemon juice, divided
Grated zest of 1 large lemon
¼ teaspoon salt plus more to taste,
   divided
¼ teaspoon pepper plus more to
   taste, divided

¼ cup extra-virgin olive oil
2 cloves garlic, mashed
4 (4- to 5- ounce) halibut fillets
2 large shallots, sliced and separated
   into rings
½ cup grapeseed oil
1 lemon, cut into 4 wedges

Combine the butter, 1 tablespoon of the lemon juice, lemon zest and ¼ teaspoon each of the salt and pepper in a bowl and mix well.

Mix the olive oil, remaining 2 tablespoons lemon juice, garlic and salt and pepper to taste in a 9×13-inch dish. Add the halibut, turning to coat evenly. Let stand for 20 minutes.

Combine the shallots and grapeseed oil in a heavy saucepan over medium-high heat. Cook for 5 to 7 minutes or until golden brown, stirring frequently; do not burn. Remove to paper towels to drain using a slotted spoon; shallots will become crisp. Season with salt and pepper.

Heat a large nonstick skillet over medium-high heat. Remove the halibut from the marinade to the skillet. Cook for 3 minutes or until seared. Turn over the fillets. Cook for 3 minutes or until seared and just until the centers are slightly pink. Remove to 4 plates. Top with equal portions of the lemon butter and shallots. Place a lemon wedge on each plate and serve.

Lime Ginger Tuna Steaks with Scallion Sauce

SERVES 4 TO 6

¼ cup peanut oil
2 tablespoons soy sauce
2 tablespoons sesame oil
Juice of ½ lime

1 tablespoon minced fresh ginger
4 cloves garlic, minced
2 pounds tuna steaks
Scallion Sauce (recipe below)

Preheat the grill to high.

Whisk the peanut oil, soy sauce, sesame oil, lime juice, ginger and garlic in a bowl until blended. Place the tuna in a sealable plastic bag. Add the marinade and turn to coat the tuna. Let stand for 20 minutes or less, turning occasionally. Grill for 2 to 3 minutes per side for rare. Serve with the Scallion Sauce on the side.

SCALLION SAUCE

4 medium scallions, chopped
1 tablespoon minced fresh ginger
2 cloves garlic, minced
2 tablespoons sesame oil

3 tablespoons hoisin sauce
2 tablespoons soy sauce
2 tablespoons lime juice
2 tablespoons black sesame seeds

Sauté the scallions, ginger and garlic in the sesame oil in a small saucepan over medium-high heat for 1 to 2 minutes. Remove from the heat. Add the hoisin sauce, soy sauce, lime juice and sesame seeds, adjusting amounts to taste. Spoon into a bowl.

Entertaining Tip

Music can really make the party! Match your playlist to the style of event and turn up the volume. Make sure there's great music playing when your guests arrive so it feels like a party when they walk through the door.

Mustard-Crusted Salmon with Lentils

SERVES 6

6 (7-ounce) salmon fillets
1½ teaspoons salt
½ teaspoon freshly ground black
  pepper

¼ cup Dijon mustard
6 teaspoons panko
2 tablespoons vegetable oil
Lentils (recipe below)

Preheat the oven to 450 degrees.

Sprinkle both sides of the salmon with the salt and pepper. Spread 2 teaspoons Dijon mustard over the rounded side of each fillet. Sprinkle each with 1 teaspoon panko, pressing into the mustard.

Heat a large ovenproof nonstick sauté pan over high heat. Add the vegetable oil. Heat until the oil begins to smoke. Add the salmon rounded side down. Reduce the heat to medium. Cook for 2 minutes or until a crust forms. Turn over the salmon. Cook for 1 minute or until seared. Bake for 3 minutes for medium-rare or 4 minutes for medium. Remove the salmon to each of 6 plates. Spoon equal portions of the Lentils onto each plate and serve.

LENTILS

1 cup green lentils
2 slices bacon, finely chopped
½ medium onion, finely chopped
1 medium carrot, finely chopped
1 rib celery, finely chopped
1 clove garlic, minced

4 sprigs of thyme, chopped
1 teaspoon salt
¼ teaspoon freshly ground
  white pepper
3 cups chicken stock

Sort and rinse the lentils in cold water. Cook the bacon in a medium saucepan over medium heat for 2 minutes or until the fat has rendered. Add the onion. Cook for 5 minutes or until the onion is translucent. Stir in the carrot, celery, garlic, thyme, salt and pepper. Cook for 5 minutes, stirring frequently. Add the stock and lentils. Bring to a simmer. Cook for 20 to 25 minutes or until the lentils are tender. Season with additional salt and pepper if needed.

Salmon with Lemon and Rosemary

SERVES 4

4 (6-ounce) salmon fillets
  (1 inch thick)
¼ cup extra-virgin olive oil
1 tablespoon minced fresh rosemary

Salt and pepper to taste
8 or 12 slices lemon
½ cup white wine
¼ cup lemon juice

Preheat the grill to medium-high.

Brush each side of the salmon fillets with the olive oil. Sprinkle with the rosemary, salt and pepper. Place each fillet on an oversized piece of heavy-duty foil, folding up the edges. Top each fillet with 2 or 3 lemon slices, 2 tablespoons wine and 1 tablespoon lemon juice. Wrap the foil securely around the fillets. Place the foil packets on the grill. Grill for 10 minutes. Remove from the foil packets before serving.

Sicilian Swordfish

SERVES 4

4 (6-ounce) swordfish steaks
  (¾ inch thick or less)
½ cup extra-virgin olive oil
6 tablespoons fresh lemon juice

4 to 5 teaspoons chopped
  fresh oregano
3 teaspoons salt

Preheat the grill to medium-high.

Grill the swordfish steaks for 3 to 4 minutes per side. Remove to a deep platter.

Combine the olive oil, lemon juice, oregano and salt in a glass jar; cover. Shake until the salt is dissolved. Poke holes all over the steaks. Pour the olive oil mixture evenly over the swordfish. Let stand to rest for 5 to 10 minutes.

DISCOVER DENVER

In 1858, a small group of prospectors arrived at the junction of Cherry Creek and the South Platte River, searching for gold. Word of their hunt quickly spread, kicking off the Colorado Gold Rush. It wasn't long before tents, tepees, wagons, and more signified the beginning of a new city. In the 1970s, the "birthplace of Denver" was converted from an industrial site to Confluence Park by the Greenway Foundation. Today, Confluence Park is a great place to take in downtown views, sunbathe, and watch kayakers brave the rapids of an urban whitewater park.

Venison with Whiskey and Herb Cream Sauce

SERVES 4

1 clove garlic, cut into halves
4 venison steaks (such as fillets, tenderloin or flank)
Salt and pepper to taste
4 tablespoons butter
1 large onion, chopped

2 cloves garlic, minced
2 cups chopped mushrooms (such as shiitake, portobello or cremini)
¼ teaspoon ground nutmeg
½ cup whiskey
1 tablespoon balsamic vinegar

¾ cup cream
1 tablespoon Dijon mustard
1 tablespoon chopped fresh rosemary

Rub the cut sides of the garlic halves over the steaks. Season generously with salt and pepper. Heat a large skillet over medium-high heat. Cook the steaks in the skillet to medium-rare, turning once. Remove to a cutting board and tent loosely with foil, reserving the drippings in the skillet. Let stand to rest.

Add the butter to the skillet drippings. Heat just until bubbly; do not scorch. Add the onion. Cook for 3 to 4 minutes, stirring frequently. Add the minced garlic. Cook for 2 minutes, reducing the heat to medium if the garlic begins to brown. Add the mushrooms. Cook for 5 minutes or until tender. Season with the nutmeg, salt and pepper. Reduce the heat to medium-low. Add the whiskey. Bring to a boil. Boil for 2 minutes. Stir in the vinegar. Boil for 2 minutes. Add the cream and mustard and mix well. Bring to a simmer. Stir in the rosemary. Simmer for 5 minutes or until slightly reduced.

Cut the steak against the grain and arrange on a serving platter. Spoon the cream sauce over the steak.

Vegetarian & Sides

Menu
Fall Harvest

Pumpkin Spice Martini ~ 49

Chorizo and Cornbread–Stuffed Mushrooms ~ 36

Spiralized Apple Salad with Citrus Dressing ~ 105

Sweet Potato Soup ~ 232

Winter Pork Roast with Port Sauce ~ 162

Roasted Cauliflower and Butternut Squash ~ 211

Apple Cranberry Crisp with Maple Whipped Cream ~ 268

Pumpkin Pie with Gingersnap Crust and
Sugared Cranberries ~ 264

Protecting Our Past

Throughout its history, the Junior League of Denver has played an essential role in the preservation and restoration of many historical sites throughout the city. From the Molly Brown House to the Paramount Theatre, many iconic Denver locations are still here today because of the hard work and vision of League volunteers. One such location is Four Mile House. Built in 1859, it is the oldest surviving home in Denver. From 1978 to 1988, League volunteers worked on research and restoration of the home, gathered oral histories, led tours, and ran a hands-on educational program for students.

Black Bean Burgers

SERVES 6

¾ cup panko
3 tablespoons plus 2 teaspoons
  extra-virgin olive oil, divided
2 (15-ounce) cans black beans, rinsed
  and drained, divided

2 large eggs
1 teaspoon ground cumin
½ teaspoon salt
¼ teaspoon cayenne pepper

1 medium red bell pepper,
  finely chopped
¼ cup fresh cilantro, minced
1 medium shallot, minced
6 brioche buns

Combine the panko and 2 teaspoons of the olive oil in a small bowl and mix with a fork. Cook in a medium skillet over medium-high heat until light golden brown, stirring frequently. Let stand to cool completely.

Mash 2½ cups of the black beans in a large bowl using a potato masher or fork until almost smooth. Combine the eggs, 1 tablespoon of the olive oil, cumin, salt and cayenne pepper in a bowl and whisk until blended. Add the egg mixture, panko, remaining ½ cup black beans, bell pepper, cilantro and shallot to the mashed black beans and mix well. Shape into 6 patties, using about ½ cup for each patty. May wrap the patties tightly with plastic wrap and chill for up to 24 hours before cooking.

Heat 1 tablespoon of the olive oil in a large skillet over medium heat until shimmery. Cook 3 of the patties in the oil for 4 to 5 minutes per side or until well browned, removing to a plate and tenting with foil to keep warm. Repeat with the remaining 1 tablespoon olive oil and 3 patties. Serve in the buns with comeback sauce or rémoulade, thick slices of smoked Gouda cheese, avocado slices, caramelized onions and leaf lettuce. May substitute pretzel buns for the brioche buns and serve with sweet pepper jelly, avocado slices, caramelized onions and spinach leaves dressed in hot chili sauce mayonnaise.

Spiced Chick-Peas and Greens

SERVES 4

1 tablespoon extra-virgin olive oil
1 yellow onion, chopped
2 tablespoons chopped fresh ginger
3 cloves garlic, minced
1 teaspoon mustard seeds

1 teaspoon ground coriander
Salt and black pepper to taste
16 ounces fresh spinach
2 (15-ounce) cans chick-peas, drained
1 (15-ounce) can coconut milk

½ cup water
1 teaspoon garam masala
2 cups rice, cooked
1 lemon, cut into wedges

Heat the olive oil in a large pot over medium heat. Cook the onion, ginger, garlic, mustard seeds, coriander, salt and pepper in the oil for 5 minutes, stirring frequently. Add the spinach. Cook for 3 minutes or until wilted, stirring frequently. Stir in the chick-peas, coconut milk, water and garam masala. Simmer for 30 minutes, stirring occasionally. Serve over the rice with lemon wedges on the side.

Baked Falafels with Tzatziki

SERVES 4

2 to 3 tablespoons extra-virgin olive oil, divided
1 (15-ounce) can chick-peas, drained
1 cup chopped white onion
½ cup fresh parsley leaves, coarsely chopped

2 cloves garlic, minced
1 egg
2 teaspoons ground cumin
1 teaspoon ground coriander
¼ teaspoon cayenne pepper
1 teaspoon lemon juice

1 teaspoon baking powder
Salt and pepper to taste
1 cup (about) bread crumbs
1 cup chopped tomatoes
2 pitas, cut into halves
Tzatziki (recipe below)

Preheat the oven to 425 degrees. Line a baking sheet with foil and coat with 1 to 2 tablespoons of the olive oil.

Mash the chick-peas in a large bowl using a fork or potato masher until thick and pasty; do not use a blender. Process the onion, parsley and garlic in a blender until smooth. Add to the chick-peas and mix well. Combine the egg, cumin, coriander, cayenne pepper, lemon juice, baking powder, salt and pepper in a small bowl and mix well. Stir the egg mixture and remaining 1 tablespoon olive oil into the chick-pea mixture. Add the bread crumbs gradually, stirring after each addition and using just enough to make the mixture hold together. Shape into 8 patties, arranging on the prepared baking sheet. Bake for 12 to 15 minutes or until the bottoms are brown. Turn over the falafels, placing in a well-oiled area. Bake for 10 minutes or until crisp on the outside and moist on the inside. Season the tomatoes with salt and pepper. Fill each pita half with 2 falafels, ¼ cup tomatoes and desired amount of Tzatziki.

TZATZIKI

6 ounces Greek yogurt
½ cup finely chopped peeled and seeded cucumber
2 or 3 cloves garlic, minced

1 tablespoon dried dill weed, or ¼ cup chopped fresh dill
½ teaspoon distilled white vinegar
½ teaspoon salt, or to taste

⅛ teaspoon white pepper, or to taste
1½ teaspoons extra-virgin olive oil (optional)

Combine the yogurt, cucumber, garlic, dill, vinegar, salt and pepper in a small bowl and mix well. Chill for 30 minutes or longer. Swirl in the olive oil just before serving.

Peruvian Savory Corn Cake with Salsa Criolla

SERVES 4 TO 6

7 cups fresh corn kernels (about 8 to 10 ears), or frozen whole kernel corn, thawed
2 teaspoons salt
½ teaspoon ground cumin
⅛ teaspoon sugar
1 to 2 tablespoons milk (optional)
1 cup medium-grind cornmeal or polenta (optional)

1¼ cups butter, softened, divided
1 cup finely chopped red onion
1 tablespoon aji amarillo hot pepper paste or habanero hot pepper sauce
4 ounces cream cheese, softened
Salsa Criolla (recipe below)

Preheat the oven to 350 degrees. Grease a 9×13-inch glass baking dish with olive oil or vegetable oil.

Process the corn, salt, cumin and sugar in a food processor or blender until smooth but grainy, adding milk if the mixture is too dry or adding cornmeal 1 tablespoon at a time if the mixture is too wet; the mixture needs to form a mound without losing its shape.

Melt 10 tablespoons of the butter in a large skillet over medium heat. Sauté the onion in the butter until tender and fragrant. Add the pepper paste. Sauté for a few minutes. Stir in the corn mixture. Cook for 2 to 3 minutes, stirring constantly. Remove from the heat. Let stand to cool slightly. Stir in the cream cheese and remaining 10 tablespoons of the butter. Spoon into the prepared baking dish. Bake, covered with foil, for 45 to 50 minutes or until the bottom is light golden brown. Let stand to cool for 10 minutes. Cut into rectangles. Serve with the Salsa Criolla.

SALSA CRIOLLA

1 cup thinly sliced red onion
1 cup thinly sliced red bell pepper
2 tablespoons lime juice
1 tablespoon chopped cilantro leaves
1 tablespoon extra-virgin olive oil or vegetable oil

Aji amarillo hot pepper paste or habanero hot pepper sauce to taste
Salt and pepper to taste

Combine the onion and enough ice water to cover in a bowl. Let stand for 10 minutes; drain well. Combine the onion, bell pepper, lime juice, cilantro, olive oil, pepper paste, salt and pepper in a bowl and mix well.

Eggplant Parmigiana

SERVES 6

5 or 6 small eggplant
1 cup all-purpose flour
3 eggs
3 to 4 tablespoons grated
    Parmesan cheese
1 teaspoon black pepper
2 cups Italian bread crumbs
Extra-virgin olive oil for frying

Tomato Sauce (recipe below)
2 cups shredded Pecorino-Romano
    cheese, or other hard Italian cheese
12 leaves fresh basil, coarsely
    chopped
1 pound fresh mozzarella cheese,
    sliced

Peel the eggplant and cut into ¼-inch slices using a mandoline if possible. Place the flour on a plate. Beat the eggs in a large bowl. Stir in the Parmesan cheese and pepper. Place the bread crumbs on a plate.

Heat about ¼ inch of olive oil in a frying pan over medium heat. Coat the eggplant in batches with the flour, egg mixture and bread crumbs. Cook in batches in the oil for 2 to 3 minutes per side or until golden brown, removing to paper towels to drain and replacing the oil after half the eggplant are cooked.

Preheat the oven to 375 degrees. Grease a 9×13-inch baking dish with nonstick cooking spray.

Layer a fourth of the Tomato Sauce, ½ cup of the Pecorino-Romano cheese, half the eggplant, half the basil, a fourth of the Tomato Sauce, ½ cup of the Pecorino-Romano cheese and half of the mozzarella cheese in the prepared baking dish. Repeat the layers, reserving a small amount of the Tomato Sauce and Pecorino-Romano cheese and ending with the remaining mozzarella cheese. Drizzle with the reserved Tomato Sauce and sprinkle with the reserved cheese. Bake, loosely covered with foil, for 30 minutes. Bake, uncovered, for 15 minutes longer or just until light brown.

TOMATO SAUCE

4 tablespoons extra-virgin olive oil
8 cloves garlic, minced
1 teaspoon red pepper flakes
3 (28-ounce) cans whole peeled
    tomatoes, crushed or diced
1 cup red wine

2 (6-ounce) cans tomato paste
¼ cup packed brown sugar
⅓ cup fresh basil, chopped
½ cup Italian parsley, chopped
1½ teaspoons salt, or to taste

Heat the olive oil in a large pot over medium heat. Sauté the garlic and red pepper flakes in the oil for 3 minutes; do not brown. Add the tomatoes and mix well. Increase the heat to medium-high. Add the wine, tomato paste, brown sugar, basil, parsley and salt and mix well. Bring to a simmer, stirring occasionally. Cook over low heat for 1 hour, stirring frequently.

Egg Roll Bowl

SERVES 6

5 cloves garlic, minced
1 teaspoon minced fresh ginger
⅓ cup soy sauce or amino acids
1 tablespoon sesame oil
1 (14-ounce) package extra-firm tofu,
   pressed and crumbled
1 tablespoon extra-virgin olive oil

4 ounces shredded cabbage or
   coleslaw mix
4 ounces shredded carrots
8 ounces kale, cut into ribbons,
   discarding ribs
1½ cups rice, cooked
1 green onion, thinly sliced

Combine the garlic, ginger, soy sauce and sesame oil in a small bowl and mix well. Sauté the tofu in the olive oil in a large skillet over high heat until brown. Reduce the heat to medium-high. Add the cabbage, carrots and kale and mix well. Stir in the garlic mixture. Cook for 3 to 5 minutes or just until the cabbage begins to wilt, stirring frequently. Serve over the rice. Sprinkle with the green onion.

Note: *May substitute 1 pound ground chicken or turkey for the tofu.*

Korean Spicy Cold Noodles

SERVES 4

1 pound soba noodles
¼ cup Korean red chili paste
   (gochujang), or more to taste
¼ cup seasoned rice vinegar
2 to 3 tablespoons soy sauce
2 tablespoons honey
2 tablespoons brown sugar
2 tablespoons toasted sesame oil
2 tablespoons black sesame seeds
2 cups romaine, thinly sliced

1 medium cucumber, peeled, seeded
   and julienned
1 medium carrot, peeled and
   julienned
1 medium Asian pear, julienned
1 bunch sesame leaves, thinly sliced
   (optional)
2 eggs, hard-boiled, peeled and cut
   into quarters

Cook the soba noodles according to the package directions for 6 to 8 minutes or until al dente; drain in a colander. Rinse with cold water and drain again.

Combine the chili paste, vinegar, soy sauce, honey, brown sugar, sesame oil and sesame seeds in small bowl and mix well. Divide the soba noodles and sauce among 4 bowls. Arrange the romaine, cucumber, carrot, pear, sesame leaves and eggs separately on a large platter, allowing guests to choose their own toppings.

Note: *Boiled shrimp may be added as one of the toppings.*

Green Chile Cheese Enchiladas

SERVES 4

1 tablespoon unsalted butter

2 ⅔ cups shredded Monterey Jack cheese or Cheddar cheese, divided

1 (4-ounce) can chopped mild green chiles

½ cup finely chopped onion

½ cup sliced black or kalamata olives

1 (15-ounce) can mild or medium green enchilada sauce

1 cup sour cream

8 corn tortillas

Preheat the oven to 400 degrees. Grease a shallow 9×13-inch baking dish with the butter.

Combine 2 cups of the Monterey Jack cheese, green chiles, onion and olives in a large bowl and mix well. Mix the enchilada sauce and sour cream in a bowl until well blended. Microwave the tortillas, wrapped in parchment paper, for 1 minute or until pliable.

Spread 1 cup of the enchilada sauce mixture over the bottom of the prepared baking dish. Fill each tortilla with ⅓ cup of the cheese mixture and roll to enclose, arranging seam side down with sides touching on top of the sauce. Sprinkle with any remaining cheese mixture. Pour the remaining enchilada sauce mixture evenly over the enchiladas, covering completely. Bake, covered, for 45 minutes or until hot and bubbly. Sprinkle with the remaining ⅔ cup Monterey Jack cheese. Bake for 10 minutes or until the cheese is melted and golden brown. Let stand for 5 to 10 minutes before serving.

Note: *One cup of chopped or shredded cooked chicken may be added to the cheese mixture, using 11 tortillas instead of 8 and using a slightly larger baking dish.*

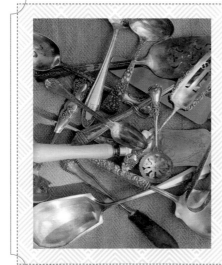

Entertaining Tip

Provide plenty of serving utensils. To keep the food line moving, be sure to stock the buffet with a spoon or set of tongs for each menu item.

Red Rocks Rellenos

SERVES 6

---

12 Anaheim or poblano peppers
8 ounces goat cheese, crumbled
8 ounces queso blanco or queso
   fresco, crumbled
2 to 3 tablespoons minced drained
   oil-packed sun-dried tomatoes

2 to 3 tablespoons chopped
   green onions
2 cloves garlic, minced
½ cup chopped fresh cilantro
½ cup chopped fresh basil
¼ teaspoon minced fresh thyme
Salt to taste

½ teaspoon ground pepper,
   or to taste
Vegetable oil
2 eggs
¼ cup heavy cream
1 to 2 cups blue cornmeal

Roast the Anaheim peppers over an open flame or under a broiler until blackened on both sides. Place in a sealable plastic bag. Let stand for 20 minutes. Peel the peppers. Cut carefully down one side and remove the seeds, leaving the stems intact. May chill the peppers in a covered container for up to 2 days.

Combine the goat cheese, queso blanco, sun-dried tomatoes, green onions, garlic, cilantro, basil and thyme in a medium bowl. Season with the salt and pepper and mix well. Fill the peppers with equal portions of the mixture, securing with wooden picks; do not overfill. May chill in a covered container until ready to bake.

Preheat the oven to 425 degrees. Line a baking sheet with foil and grease lightly with vegetable oil.

Beat the eggs and cream in a bowl. Spread the cornmeal on parchment paper. Dip the filled peppers in the egg mixture and coat evenly with the cornmeal, arranging on the prepared baking sheet. Bake for 15 minutes. Turn over the peppers using a large metal spatula. Bake for 15 minutes longer. Serve with salsa and sliced avocados.

Note: *The rellenos may be broiled for 7 minutes per side instead of baking. Anaheim peppers are usually spicier than poblano peppers. Choose accordingly.*

Spinach and Goat Cheese Pie

SERVES 6

1 cup extra-virgin olive oil, divided
3 cups chopped yellow onions
½ cup chopped fresh dill, or
    ¼ cup dried
½ cup chopped fresh Italian parsley,
    or ¼ cup dried
1½ teaspoons salt, or to taste

1 tablespoon ground black pepper
32 ounces fresh spinach, coarsely
    chopped
1 (16-ounce) package frozen phyllo
    dough, thawed
4 to 6 ounces crumbled goat cheese

Preheat the oven to 375 degrees. Grease a 9×13-inch baking dish lightly.

Heat ½ cup of the olive oil in a large stockpot over medium heat. Sauté the onions, dill, parsley, salt and pepper in the oil for 10 minutes or until the onion is translucent. Add the spinach in batches, cooking until wilted after each addition and stirring frequently, for a total of 10 to 12 minutes; drain if needed. May be made ahead and chilled, covered, overnight.

Layer 7 sheets of the phyllo dough in the prepared baking dish, covering the sides of the dish and basting each layer with a small amount of the remaining ½ cup olive oil. Layer with the spinach mixture and goat cheese. Layer with 7 sheets of the phyllo dough, basting each layer with a small amount of the remaining olive oil. Fold over the excess dough from the sides and brush with olive oil. Bake for 25 to 30 minutes or until brown, hot and bubbly.

Palak Paneer

SERVES 6

2 serrano peppers
3 cloves garlic
1½ tablespoons minced fresh ginger,
    divided
2 large white or yellow onions,
    coarsely chopped
¼ cup extra-virgin olive oil or canola oil

5 teaspoons ground cumin
2 teaspoons ground coriander
2 teaspoons ground turmeric
1 cup sour cream or Greek yogurt
24 ounces fresh spinach
1 large tomato, cut into fourths
1 cup chopped fresh cilantro

1½ teaspoons salt, or to taste
1 teaspoon cayenne pepper,
    or to taste
8 ounces paneer, cut into
    ½-inch cubes

Chop the serrano peppers, garlic and 1 tablespoon of the ginger finely in a food processor. Remove to a bowl. Cook the onions in the olive oil in a large nonstick sauté pan over medium-low heat for 20 minutes, stirring frequently. Add the serrano pepper mixture. Cook for 30 seconds. Stir in the cumin, coriander, turmeric and sour cream. Add the spinach by the handful. Cook until wilted, stirring frequently. Let stand to cool. Process the spinach mixture, tomato, cilantro and remaining ½ tablespoon ginger in a food processor until smooth. Return to the saucepan. Cook over low heat for 10 minutes, adding the salt and cayenne pepper and stirring frequently. Stir in the paneer. Serve over rice or with naan or paratha.

Fried Green Tomatoes with Goat Cheese Fondue

SERVES 4 TO 6

2 cups buttermilk
½ cup grated Parmigiano-Reggiano
   cheese
3 tablespoons finely chopped
   fresh ginger

3 tablespoons minced garlic
1 tablespoon dried oregano
1 tablespoon dried thyme
2 large green tomatoes, cut into
   ¼-inch slices

2 cups cornmeal
2 tablespoons salt
2 cups peanut oil
Goat Cheese Fondue
   (recipe below)

Process the buttermilk, Parmigiano-Reggiano cheese, ginger, garlic, oregano and thyme in a blender until well mixed. Pour over the tomatoes in a large bowl. Chill, covered, for 4 hours. Mix the cornmeal and salt in a shallow bowl. Coat the tomatoes with the cornmeal mixture. May let the tomatoes stand for up to 1 hour. Deep-fry the tomatoes in the peanut oil at 350 degrees in a saucepan or deep-fryer until golden brown. Place 2 or 3 fried green tomatoes on individual serving plates. Serve with the Goat Cheese Fondue.

GOAT CHEESE FONDUE

2 cups low-sodium vegetable broth
2 cups canned San Marzano
   tomatoes
1 cup roasted cherry tomatoes
   (see Note)

2 ounces tomato paste
1 cup heavy cream
5 cloves garlic
½ cup chopped shallots
½ cup chopped fresh basil

2 tablespoons unsalted butter
1 tablespoon extra-virgin olive oil
8 ounces goat cheese, broken
   into pieces

Combine the broth, San Marzano tomatoes, cherry tomatoes, tomato paste, cream, garlic, shallots, basil, butter and olive oil in a pot. Simmer over low heat until reduced by a third, stirring frequently. Process in a blender until smooth. Return to the pot. Add the goat cheese. Simmer for 5 minutes or until the cheese is melted, stirring until smooth.

Note: *To roast cherry tomatoes for the fondue, toss the tomatoes with olive oil and spread on a baking sheet. Roast in the oven at 400 degrees for 15 to 20 minutes or until the skins are loose and mostly brown.*

Tomato Pie with Basil and Gruyère

SERVES 6

2 ¼ cups unbleached
   all-purpose flour
3 teaspoons salt, divided
1 cup cold unsalted butter, cut
   into cubes
¾ cup sour cream

5 to 8 tablespoons ice water
2 ½ pounds assorted red and
   yellow tomatoes, divided
1 ¾ cups grated Gruyère cheese
½ cup grated Parmesan cheese
¾ cup mayonnaise

1 egg, beaten
½ cup loosely packed fresh basil
   leaves, cut into chiffonade
1 tablespoon chopped fresh thyme
¼ teaspoon pepper
1 cup chopped sweet yellow onion

Process the flour and 1 teaspoon of the salt in a food processor just until blended. Add the butter and pulse until the mixture resembles coarse meal. Remove to a bowl. Mix in the sour cream. Add the ice water 1 tablespoon at a time, mixing by hand until the dough forms a ball. Knead the dough 4 or 5 times. Wrap in plastic wrap and chill for 30 minutes.

Roll out the dough into a 13-inch circle on a floured surface. Fit into a 9-inch fluted tart pan with 2-inch sides and a removable bottom, trimming the edge. Chill for 30 minutes.

Cut the tomatoes into ¼-inch slices and remove the seeds. Reserve ½ pound of the tomato slices. Arrange the remaining slices on paper towels. Sprinkle with 1 teaspoon of the salt. Let stand for 30 minutes. Pat dry with paper towels.

Preheat the oven to 425 degrees.

Combine the Gruyère cheese, Parmesan cheese, mayonnaise, egg, basil, thyme, remaining 1 teaspoon salt and pepper in a bowl and mix well.

Spread the onion over the bottom of the pie shell. Dollop a third of the cheese mixture over the onion. Arrange half of the salted tomatoes over the cheese mixture, overlapping the slices. Repeat the layers of cheese mixture and tomatoes. Dollop with the remaining cheese mixture. Top with the reserved tomatoes, overlapping the slices.

Place the pie on a baking sheet. Bake for 40 to 45 minutes or until the crust is brown and the filling is hot and bubbly, covering the outer rim of the crust with a foil ring or crust shield if the crust browns too quickly. Let stand at room temperature to cool completely. Garnish with basil chiffonade.

Summer Vegetable Ratatouille over Polenta

SERVES 6

1 medium red onion, thinly sliced
1 red bell pepper, thinly sliced
2 tablespoons extra-virgin olive oil
1 medium eggplant, thinly sliced

1 medium zucchini, thinly sliced
1 pint cherry tomatoes,
 cut into halves
Italian seasoning to taste

Salt and pepper to taste
Parmesan Polenta (recipe below)
Chopped fresh Italian parsley
Shredded Parmesan cheese

Sauté the onion and bell pepper in the olive oil in a skillet over medium heat for 3 minutes. Add the eggplant and zucchini. Sauté for 3 minutes. Increase the heat to medium-high. Add the cherry tomatoes. Cook for 5 to 7 minutes or until the vegetables are tender, stirring occasionally. Season with Italian seasoning, salt and pepper. Serve over the Parmesan Polenta and sprinkle with parsley and Parmesan cheese.

PARMESAN POLENTA

1 cup dried polenta
⅓ cup grated Parmesan cheese
5 cloves garlic, minced

1 teaspoon Italian seasoning
⅛ teaspoon red pepper flakes
Salt and pepper to taste

Cook the polenta according to the package directions until thickened. Remove from the heat. Stir in the Parmesan cheese, garlic, Italian seasoning, red pepper flakes, salt and pepper.

Roasted Vegetables with Black Rice

SERVES 4

2 cups canned chick-peas, well rinsed
 and drained
1 cup peeled coarsely chopped
 sweet potato
1½ cups chopped broccoli

1 cup peeled coarsely
 chopped carrots
1 cup coarsely chopped green
 bell pepper
1 tablespoon extra-virgin olive oil
1 teaspoon ground cumin

1½ teaspoons onion powder
1½ teaspoons garlic powder
1 teaspoon ground turmeric
1½ teaspoons salt, or to taste
Cayenne pepper to taste
1 cup black rice, cooked

Preheat the oven to 375 degrees. Line a baking sheet with foil.

Combine the chick-peas, sweet potato, broccoli, carrots and bell pepper in a large bowl. Mix the olive oil, cumin, onion powder, garlic powder, turmeric, salt and cayenne pepper in a small bowl. Pour over the chick-pea mixture and stir to coat. Spread in a single layer on the prepared baking sheet. Roast for 20 to 25 minutes or until the sweet potato and carrots are tender. Return to the large bowl. Add the rice and toss to mix. Season with salt, black pepper and cayenne pepper if needed. Divide among 4 plates and serve.

SUMMER VEGETABLE RATATOUILLE

Vegetarian Bibimbap

SERVES 4

---

3 to 6 tablespoons sesame oil, divided
1 cup matchstick-cut carrots
1 cup matchstick-cut zucchini
1 cup matchstick-cut red or yellow
   bell pepper (optional)
1 cup thinly sliced red onion (optional)
1 or 2 cloves garlic, minced

2 cups fresh shiitake mushrooms,
   sliced
4 cups fresh bean sprouts (about
   8 ounces), or 1 (14-ounce) can
   bean sprouts, drained
1 (5-ounce) can bamboo shoots,
   drained (optional)

¼ cup sweet red chili sauce,
   or to taste
⅛ teaspoon salt plus more to taste
2 to 3 tablespoons butter
4 eggs
Pepper to taste
Seasoned Rice (recipe below)

Heat 2 tablespoons of the sesame oil in a large skillet over medium heat. Cook the carrots, zucchini, bell pepper, onion and garlic in the oil for 5 to 7 minutes or just until tender, adding 1 tablespoon more oil if adding the optional ingredients. Add 1 tablespoon of the sesame oil. Stir in the mushrooms and fresh bean sprouts (if using canned bean sprouts, add with the bamboo shoots). Cook for 5 to 7 minutes or just until the mushrooms and bean sprouts are tender. Stir in the bamboo shoots and chili sauce. Cook until heated through, stirring constantly. Season with ⅛ teaspoon salt. Keep the mixture warm.

Melt the butter in a skillet over medium heat. Fry the eggs in the butter for 2 to 3 minutes or until the egg whites are firm and the yolks are slightly runny. Season with salt and pepper to taste. Divide the Seasoned Rice and vegetable mixture evenly among 4 individual serving bowls. Top each with a fried egg. Drizzle with the desired amount of the remaining sesame oil. Serve with additional chili sauce.

SEASONED RICE

1⅓ cups short or medium grain rice
½ cup chopped green onions

2 tablespoons soy sauce
¼ teaspoon crushed black pepper

Cook the rice according to the package directions. Stir in the green onions, soy sauce and pepper; cover. Turn off the heat. Keep warm.

Note: *With traditional bibimbap, a stronger sauce is used and the vegetables are placed individually on a plate for the guests to make their own mixture.*

Vegetarian Casserole

SERVES 6

2 tablespoons extra-virgin olive oil
½ medium onion, chopped
2 cloves garlic, minced
6 cups chopped kale
Salt and pepper to taste

½ cup plus 3 tablespoons
   vegetable broth, divided
2 cups chopped butternut squash
2 cups chopped zucchini
1 cup shredded potatoes
½ cup quinoa

2 tablespoons mayonnaise
1 egg
½ cup grated Parmesan cheese plus
   more to taste, divided
½ cup shredded Pepper Jack cheese

Preheat the oven to 400 degrees. Grease a 9×9-inch or 2-quart baking dish.

Heat the olive oil in a large nonstick skillet over medium heat. Cook the onion in the oil for 5 minutes or just until tender and brown, stirring occasionally. Add the garlic. Cook for 2 to 3 minutes, stirring occasionally. Add the kale, salt and pepper. Cook for 2 minutes or until the kale is bright green. Stir in ½ cup of the broth. Cook for 5 minutes or until the kale is wilted and most of the broth is absorbed.

Add the butternut squash, zucchini, potatoes, salt and pepper and mix well. Cook for 8 minutes or just until the butternut squash is tender.

Add the quinoa and mix well, adding the remaining 3 tablespoons broth if the mixture is too dry. Spoon into a large bowl. Stir in the mayonnaise, egg, ½ cup of the Parmesan cheese and Pepper Jack cheese.

Spread the mixture in the prepared baking dish. Sprinkle with Parmesan cheese to taste. Bake for 35 minutes or until the butternut squash and zucchini are very tender and the top is brown and crisp. Serve hot with hot sauce on the side.

DISCOVER DENVER

Built in 1914, this historic landmark is home to some of downtown Denver's best shops, restaurants, and bars.

Ginger Soy Bok Choy

SERVES 4

3 bunches baby bok choy
1 tablespoon sugar
1 tablespoon salt
1 cup soy sauce

¾ cup packed dark brown sugar
2 tablespoons minced garlic
1 tablespoon rice wine vinegar
1 tablespoon hot chili sauce

1½ teaspoons ground black pepper
1 teaspoon grated fresh ginger
1 teaspoon toasted sesame oil

Separate the bok choy into leaves. Tear each leaf carefully into 3 or 4 bite-size squares. Combine the bok choy, sugar and salt in a bowl, rubbing the sugar and salt into the leaves. Let stand for 40 minutes or until wilted and brined.

Combine the soy sauce, brown sugar, garlic, vinegar, chili sauce, pepper, ginger and sesame oil in a saucepan. Bring to a boil. Simmer over low heat until reduced by a fourth; do not boil over.

Rinse the bok choy under cold water; drain and pat dry. Place in a serving bowl. Pour the soy sauce mixture over the bok choy. Serve immediately or chill until serving time.

Note: *If you don't want to brine the bok choy, you may julienne the leaves, dress with the soy sauce mixture and serve as a warm salad.*

Roasted Broccoli and Green Beans with Asiago Cheese

SERVES 6

4 bunches broccoli
8 ounces French green beans
¼ cup avocado oil
⅓ cup shredded asiago cheese, divided
Juice of 1 medium lemon, divided
1 teaspoon salt, divided

¼ teaspoon freshly ground black pepper
9 ounces strawberry or cherry tomatoes, cut into halves
4 to 6 cloves garlic, minced
2 tablespoons chiffonade-cut fresh basil

Preheat the oven to 400 degrees, placing the oven rack at the center position.

Trim the broccoli and green beans, breaking the broccoli into florets. Arrange the broccoli and green beans on a baking sheet. Drizzle with the avocado oil. Sprinkle with half the asiago cheese, half the lemon juice, ½ teaspoon of the salt and pepper. Bake for 20 minutes. Turn the vegetables over. Add the tomatoes and garlic. Bake for 20 minutes longer. Sprinkle with the remaining ½ teaspoon salt, remaining half of the lemon juice, basil and remaining half of the asiago cheese.

Roasted Butternut Squash with Baby Spinach and Cranberries

SERVES 6

2 large butternut squash
1 medium red onion, peeled
  and chopped
3 tablespoons Basting Oil
  (recipe below)

Salt and pepper to taste
1 (6-ounce) package fresh
  baby spinach
¾ cup dried cranberries

Preheat the oven to 400 degrees. Line a baking sheet with parchment paper.

Peel and seed the butternut squash and cut into 1-inch pieces. Combine the butternut squash and onion in a large bowl. Drizzle with the Basting Oil and toss to coat. Season with salt and pepper. Arrange in a single layer on the prepared baking sheet. Roast for 35 minutes or until light brown and tender. Add the spinach and dried cranberries and toss to mix. Remove to a serving bowl.

BASTING OIL

½ cup extra-virgin olive oil
1 clove garlic, crushed

1 teaspoon dried parsley flakes
½ teaspoon dried thyme

Combine the olive oil, garlic, parsley and thyme in a jar with a lid or in a bowl. Shake or stir until blended.

Maple Roasted Brussels Sprouts

SERVES 4 TO 6

2 pounds brussels sprouts, trimmed
  and cut into halves
4 tablespoons unsalted butter, melted
1¼ teaspoons kosher salt, divided
¼ teaspoon garlic powder
3 slices bacon
1 tablespoon unsalted butter

1 medium Granny Smith apple, cut
  into 1-inch matchstick slices
1 teaspoon apple cider vinegar
1 small clove garlic, minced
1 tablespoon maple syrup
Freshly cracked black pepper to taste

Preheat the oven to 400 degrees. Line a baking sheet with parchment paper or use a nonstick baking sheet.

Place the brussels sprouts in a large bowl. Add the melted butter, ¾ teaspoon of the salt and garlic powder and toss to mix. Spread on the prepared baking sheet. Bake for 15 to 20 minutes or until golden brown.

Cook the bacon in a large sauté pan over medium heat until crisp. Remove to a plate, reserving 1 tablespoon drippings in the pan. Add 1 tablespoon butter to the drippings. Crumble the bacon into the drippings. Add the brussels sprouts, apple, vinegar and minced garlic. Cook until heated through, stirring frequently. Stir in the maple syrup, remaining ½ teaspoon salt and pepper. Serve immediately.

Rainbow Carrots with Avocado

SERVES 4 TO 6

1½ pounds multi-colored carrots
½ teaspoon salt plus more to taste
2 teaspoons ground cumin
2 teaspoons ground coriander
1 teaspoon dried thyme
⅛ teaspoon red pepper flakes, crushed

3 cloves garlic, minced
¼ cup plus 2 tablespoons extra-virgin olive oil
2 tablespoons balsamic or red wine vinegar
Pepper to taste
1 large avocado, thinly sliced

1 cup arugula
3 tablespoons orange juice
Tahini Sauce (recipe below)
2 tablespoons pistachios, coarsely chopped

Preheat the oven to 400 degrees. Line a baking sheet with aluminum foil.

Peel the carrots if desired. Cut lengthwise into halves and crosswise into 3-inch pieces. Bring enough water to cover the carrots and ½ teaspoon salt to a boil over high heat. Add the carrots. Cook for 5 minutes. Drain in a colander, shaking to remove any excess water. Spread the carrots on the prepared baking sheet.

Combine the cumin, coriander, thyme and red pepper flakes in a jar with a lid and shake to mix. Add the garlic, ¼ cup of the olive oil and vinegar and shake to mix well. Season with salt and pepper to taste. Pour evenly over the carrots and toss to coat, spreading in a single layer. Roast for 20 minutes or just until the carrots are golden brown and tender. Arrange on a serving platter. Arrange the avocado and arugula over the carrots. Mix the orange juice and remaining 2 tablespoons olive oil in a small bowl. Season with salt and pepper to taste. Drizzle over the carrot mixture. Add a few spoonfuls of the Tahini Sauce. Sprinkle with the pistachios. Serve immediately.

TAHINI SAUCE

⅓ cup sour cream or Greek yogurt
2 tablespoons tahini
⅛ teaspoon salt

Combine the sour cream, tahini and salt in a bowl and mix well. Chill until serving time.

Roasted Cauliflower and Butternut Squash

SERVES 6 TO 8

1 head cauliflower
1 large butternut squash
Vegetable or canola oil to taste
1 tablespoon dried oregano
1 tablespoon Italian seasoning
Kosher salt to taste

Sweet and Spicy Dressing
　(recipe below)
2 cups arugula
½ cup crumbled feta cheese
　(optional)
Black pepper to taste

Preheat the oven to 400 degrees. Line 2 baking sheets with foil.

Cut the cauliflower into 1-inch florets. Spread on 1 of the baking sheets. Peel and seed the butternut squash and cut into 1-inch pieces. Spread on the remaining baking sheet. Drizzle the cauliflower and squash with vegetable oil and toss to coat. Spread each in an even layer. Combine the oregano, Italian seasoning and salt in a small bowl and mix well. Sprinkle evenly over the cauliflower and squash. Roast for 30 to 45 minutes or until tender and golden brown; the cauliflower may take less time than the squash.

Combine the cauliflower and squash in a large bowl or platter and toss to mix. Drizzle with the Sweet and Spicy Dressing and toss to coat. Fold in the arugula. Sprinkle with the feta cheese. Season with additional salt and black pepper if needed.

SWEET AND SPICY DRESSING

3 tablespoons extra-virgin olive oil
3 tablespoons canola oil
2 tablespoons red wine vinegar
1½ tablespoons molasses
¼ teaspoon cayenne pepper
Salt and black pepper to taste

Whisk the olive oil, canola oil, vinegar, molasses, cayenne pepper, salt and black pepper in a bowl until well blended.

Cauliflower Grits

SERVES 4 TO 6

1 head cauliflower
1 cup (about) coconut milk, divided
¼ cup vegetable stock or unsalted chicken stock
1 tablespoon unsalted butter

¼ teaspoon kosher salt plus more to taste
¼ cup grated Parmesan cheese
Cayenne pepper to taste (optional)
Black pepper to taste

Grate the cauliflower or process in a food processor until the size of rice, making 4 cups. Sauté in a medium sauté pan over medium-high heat for 5 minutes or until some of the moisture is released. Stir in ¼ cup of the coconut milk, stock, butter and ¼ teaspoon salt. Cook for 5 minutes or until the cauliflower is tender and the liquid is absorbed, stirring constantly. Process with an immersion blender or blender until the consistency of grits; do not overprocess. Return to medium heat. Add the Parmesan cheese. Cook until the cheese is melted, stirring constantly. Add the remaining coconut milk gradually, stirring constantly and using just enough coconut milk to make the grits smooth and creamy. Season with cayenne pepper, salt and black pepper to taste.

Note: *Cauliflower Grits are pictured on page 171 as an accompaniment to Champagne Shrimp.*

Loaded Cauliflower

SERVES 4 TO 6

1 large head cauliflower, cored
2 cups sharp Cheddar cheese
½ cup mayonnaise
½ cup sour cream

1 (4-ounce) package crumbled cooked bacon (not imitation bacon bits)
6 tablespoons chopped chives
Salt and pepper to taste

Preheat the oven to 350 degrees.

Combine the cauliflower and a small amount of water in a microwave-safe bowl; cover loosely with a paper towel. Microwave the cauliflower for 5 minutes; drain. Break the cauliflower into small florets, discarding the stems.

Add the Cheddar cheese, mayonnaise, sour cream, bacon, chives, salt and pepper to the cauliflower and mix well. Spoon into a baking dish. Bake for 30 minutes or until the cauliflower is tender and the sauce is hot and bubbly.

Turkish Eggplant with Walnuts and Garlic

SERVES 6

2 to 3 tablespoons (or more) extra-virgin olive oil, divided
2 pounds eggplant
2 to 3 tablespoons red wine vinegar

¼ to ½ teaspoon kosher salt plus more to taste
6 or 7 cloves garlic, crushed
½ cup walnuts
1 bunch Italian parsley

Preheat the oven to 475 degrees. Line a baking sheet with foil. Grease the foil lightly with olive oil.

Cut the eggplant lengthwise into ¼- to ½-inch slices. Brush both sides of the slices with a small amount of olive oil, arranging on the prepared baking sheet. Bake for 10 minutes. Turn over the eggplant. Bake for 10 minutes longer or until tender and golden brown. Arrange the eggplant in a single layer on a serving platter. Season with the vinegar and salt to taste.

Cook the garlic in 1 tablespoon of the olive oil in a small frying pan over medium heat until tender and fragrant, stirring constantly; do not brown. Remove from the heat. Process the walnuts in a food processor until finely chopped. Add the garlic, parsley, remaining 1 to 2 tablespoons olive oil and ¼ to ½ teaspoon salt and pulse to mix. Spread over the eggplant. Serve at room temperature or chilled; may be made 1 day ahead.

Note: *The eggplant may be brushed with olive oil and grilled on a lightly oiled rack for 6 to 8 minutes per side or until tender and slightly charred around the edges.*

Garlic Braised Greens

SERVES 4 TO 6

1 quart Tuscan kale (such as lacinato kale)
1 quart Swiss chard
1 quart collard greens
2 tablespoons extra-virgin olive oil

4 teaspoons minced garlic, divided
2 cups chicken broth
Lemon juice to taste
Kosher salt and pepper to taste

Cut the leaves of the kale, chard and collard greens into bite-size pieces, placing in a colander. Rinse thoroughly and drain well.

Sauté the kale, chard and collard greens in the olive oil in a large pot over medium heat for 3 minutes or until heated through and sizzling. Stir in the garlic. Add the broth and mix well. Bring to a boil. Simmer over low heat for 30 to 45 minutes or until most of the liquid has evaporated, stirring and tasting frequently to determine doneness; drain if needed. Season with lemon juice, salt and pepper.

Grilled Corn with Cotija and Lime

SERVES 10

10 ears corn in husks
¾ cup unsalted butter, softened
1 teaspoon cayenne pepper
1 teaspoon chili powder
Juice and grated zest of
   1 medium lime, divided

¾ cup crumbled Cotija cheese
¼ cup loosely packed cilantro,
   chopped
Salt and freshly ground pepper
   to taste

Peel back the husks from the corn just to the base. Remove and discard the silks. Tie the husks with cooking twine to form handles. Soak the corn in enough water to cover the husks in a pan for 10 minutes.

Preheat the grill to medium-high.

Remove the corn from the water and shake to remove any excess water. Pat the kernels dry. Grill over direct heat for 10 to 12 minutes or until tender and light brown, turning frequently. Remove to a platter.

Combine the butter, cayenne pepper, chili powder and lime juice in a small bowl. Spread over the corn. Sprinkle the corn with the Cotija cheese, cilantro, lime zest, salt and pepper. Serve immediately.

DISCOVER DENVER

John and Mary Elitch opened Elitch Gardens in Northwest Denver in 1890 as a botanic garden, which included the Elitch Theater and the first zoo west of Chicago. When her husband died the year after the park opened, Mary became the first woman in the United States to own and manage a zoo, as well as run a theater. In the 1930s, the emphasis shifted from the zoo and gardens to rides and entertainment. In 1995, "Elitch's" became an iconic part of the Denver skyline when the majority of the rides were relocated to its new home along the South Platte River in downtown Denver.

Tequila and Lime–Pickled Pineapple and Fennel

SERVES 10

1 cup distilled white vinegar
3 tablespoons tequila
3 tablespoons lime juice
3 tablespoons sugar
1½ teaspoons salt
1 teaspoon fennel seeds ·
½ pineapple
1 small fennel bulb, cored and
   thinly sliced

1 jalapeño, seeded and thinly sliced
2 tablespoons chopped fresh cilantro
   (optional)
2 tablespoons chopped fresh mint
   (optional)
Grated zest of 1 medium lime
Coarsely ground pepper to taste

Combine the vinegar, tequila, lime juice, sugar, salt and fennel seeds in a small saucepan. Bring to a boil. Cook until the sugar is dissolved, stirring frequently. Let stand to cool for 15 minutes.

Peel and core the pineapple. Cut lengthwise into halves or thirds. Cut into ¼-inch slices. Combine the pineapple, fennel and jalapeño in a bowl. Add the vinegar mixture and stir to coat. Let stand for 2 hours, stirring occasionally. Chill, covered, for up to 5 days; the mixture will get spicier the longer it is kept. Sprinkle servings with cilantro, mint, lime zest and ground pepper. May sprinkle with additional jalapeño slices if desired.

Entertaining Tip

Look no further than your yard or environment for decor inspiration! Forage simple cuts of greenery sprigs, berries, or grasses for a beautiful combination to make a seasonal centerpiece. Also, support your local flower farmers. Flowers often travel miles in planes and trucks from South America and Holland. Buying locally reduces the industry carbon footprint and supports the efforts of your hometown gardeners.

Potato Gratin with Gournay Cheese

SERVES 8 TO 10

1 tablespoon butter
2 pounds red new potatoes
2 cups heavy whipping cream
5 ounces Gournay cheese with garlic
  and fine herbs (such as Boursin®)

6 tablespoons freshly grated
  Parmesan cheese
Salt and black pepper to taste
1½ tablespoons minced fresh
  Italian parsley

Preheat the oven to 400 degrees. Coat the bottom and sides of a 9×13-inch baking dish with the butter.

Scrub the new potatoes and cut into thin slices using a mandolin if possible.

Combine the cream and Gournay cheese in a small saucepan. Cook over medium heat until the cheese is melted, stirring frequently to blend. Layer a third of the potatoes, 3 tablespoons of the Parmesan cheese and a third of the cream mixture in the prepared baking dish. Season generously with salt and pepper. Repeat the layers of potatoes, Parmesan cheese and cream mixture. Season generously with salt and pepper. Add the remaining potatoes and remaining cream mixture. Season generously with salt and pepper.

Bake, covered with foil, for 1 hour or until the potatoes are almost tender. Increase the oven temperature to 425 degrees. Bake, uncovered, until brown and the potatoes are tender. Sprinkle with the parsley and serve.

DISCOVER DENVER

The blue columbine was officially designated the Colorado state flower in 1899. The blue represents the Colorado sky. The white represents snow. The yellow honors Colorado's gold mining history.

Roasted Potato Wedges

SERVES 10

6 medium russet potatoes, scrubbed
¼ cup extra-virgin olive oil
6 cloves garlic, minced
2 teaspoons salt
1 teaspoon black pepper

1 teaspoon crushed dried rosemary
1 teaspoon dried oregano
1 teaspoon dried thyme
1 teaspoon paprika

Preheat the oven to 425 degrees. Line a baking sheet with foil.

Cut each potato lengthwise into halves. Cut each half lengthwise into fourths. Combine the potatoes, olive oil, garlic, salt, pepper, rosemary, oregano, thyme and paprika in a large bowl or sealable plastic bag. Toss or shake for a few minutes or until the potatoes are well coated. Arrange the potatoes skin side down on the prepared baking sheet. Bake for 30 to 40 minutes or until tender, well browned and crusty. Serve immediately.

Pesto Parmesan Summer Squash

SERVES 4 TO 6

4 teaspoons avocado oil
4 to 6 summer squash or zucchini
1 teaspoon Italian seasoning

Salt and pepper to taste
⅓ cup basil pesto
½ cup shredded Parmesan cheese

Preheat the oven to 450 degrees. Brush or spray a baking sheet with a small amount of the avocado oil.

Cut the squash into ½-inch slices. Arrange in a single layer on the prepared baking sheet. Brush with the remaining avocado oil. Sprinkle with the Italian seasoning, salt and pepper. Roast for 10 minutes or until tender. Brush with the basil pesto and sprinkle with the Parmesan cheese. Broil for 3 to 4 minutes or until the cheese is melted and light brown.

Soups & Sandwiches

Menu

Après Anything

WINTER

Mayan Mocha ~ 55

Orange Rosemary Gin Rickey ~ 49

Roasted Vegetable and Gournay Grilled Cheese
Sandwiches ~ 241

Slow Cooker Tomato and Carrot Soup ~ 235

Vanilla Bean Marshmallows ~ 287

Après All These Years

Since its founding in 1918, the Junior League of Denver has awarded nearly $2 million in grants to hundreds of organizations in the Denver community, such as the Women's Foundation of Colorado, Anchor Center for Blind Children, SafeHouse Denver, and the Mile High Transplant Bank. The League has also invested millions of dollars in its own community programs and sponsorships. Thanks to these grants, programs, and the hard work of its trained volunteer workforce, the League has been tackling the critical needs of women and children in the community for more than a century.

Fajita Soup

SERVES 2 TO 4

2 frozen large boneless skinless
    chicken breasts, partially thawed
1 large sweet onion
½ green bell pepper
½ red bell pepper
½ yellow bell pepper
1 large poblano pepper

2 tablespoons extra-virgin olive oil
½ teaspoon ground cumin
½ teaspoon onion powder
¼ teaspoon garlic powder
Salt and pepper to taste
1 heaping tablespoon chili powder
2 or 3 drops hot pepper sauce

2 cups chopped fresh tomatoes
½ cup water
1¾ cups chicken broth or stock
Shredded Mexican-blend cheese
    to taste

Cut the chicken, onion, green bell pepper, red bell pepper, yellow bell pepper and poblano pepper into strips. Heat a soup pot over medium-high heat. Add the olive oil, chicken, onion, bell peppers and poblano pepper. Sprinkle with the cumin, onion powder, garlic powder, salt and pepper and mix well. Stir in the chili powder and pepper sauce. Cook until the chicken begins to brown, stirring occasionally. Add the tomatoes and water. Cook over high heat until bubbly. Stir in the broth. Bring to a boil. Simmer over medium-low heat for 30 minutes, stirring occasionally. Ladle into soup bowls and sprinkle with Mexican-blend cheese.

Desroches Island Chili con Carne

SERVES 6

1 pound ground beef
3 to 4 cloves garlic, minced
2 poblano peppers, seeded and
    chopped

2 teaspoons dried oregano
2 teaspoons tomato paste
1 (28-ounce) can crushed tomatoes
1 cup kidney beans

1 cup sweet corn kernels
4⅓ cups beef stock
Salt to taste
Hot pepper sauce to taste

Brown the ground beef in a heavy casserole pot, stirring to crumble; drain. Stir in the garlic, poblano peppers and oregano. Sauté until fragrant. Add the tomato paste to the center of the pot. Cook over medium-low heat for 3 to 4 minutes without stirring. Stir into the ground beef mixture. Add the tomatoes, kidney beans, corn and stock and mix well. Season with salt and pepper sauce. Cook for 1 to 1½ hours or until the sauce is thickened, stirring occasionally.

Chili Blanco Especial

Favorite recipe from Crème de Colorado *chosen by Chairman and Editor Connie Hambrook*

SERVES 8

1 pound dry Great Northern beans
7 cups chicken broth, divided
1 large white onion, chopped
2 cloves garlic, minced
1 tablespoon dried oregano

1 tablespoon ground cumin
1 tablespoon ground white pepper
1 teaspoon salt
½ teaspoon ground cloves
5 cups diced cooked chicken breasts

1 (7-ounce) can diced green chiles
1 tablespoon chopped jalapeño
  (optional)
8 flour tortillas

Soak the beans in enough water to cover in a covered bowl for 24 hours; drain. Combine the beans, 5¼ cups of the broth, onion, garlic, oregano, cumin, white pepper, salt and cloves in slow cooker or large soup pot. Simmer, covered, for 5 hours or until the beans are tender, stirring occasionally.

Stir in the chicken, green chiles, jalapeño and remaining 1¾ cups broth. Simmer, covered, for 1 hour. Linc each of 8 soup bowls with a tortilla. Ladle the soup into the bowls. Serve with shredded Monterey Jack cheese, sliced black olives, chunky salsa, sour cream and chopped avocado.

Crème de Colorado represents the best of Colorado cooking, reaching beyond the realm of the ordinary cookbook. Readers enjoy fifteen sections of scrumptious recipes ranging from Wild Duck Gumbo to sensational Chicken Fajitas. *Crème* has been a smash hit since its publication in 1988.

Congresswoman Pat Schroeder entered a chili made from a recipe in *Crème de Colorado* in the Congressional Club's annual chili cook-off and won!

Spicy Tomatillo Chicken Soup

SERVES 4

1 pound tomatillos, husks removed
1 pound yellow cherry tomatoes
¼ cup cilantro plus more to taste, divided
1 tablespoon extra-virgin olive oil
1 medium yellow onion, chopped
1 large jalapeño, seeded and finely chopped

1 medium Anaheim or Hatch pepper, seeded and finely chopped
4 cloves garlic, minced
1 teaspoon ground cumin
1 pound ground chicken, cooked and crumbled
2 cups chicken broth

Salt and pepper to taste
Chili oil to taste
Tortilla chips
Sour cream

Preheat the oven to 375 degrees. Line a baking sheet with foil and spray with nonstick cooking spray.

Cut the tomatillos into halves. Arrange the tomatillos and tomatoes on the prepared baking sheet. Roast for 20 minutes or until tender. Let stand to cool for 5 minutes. Process the tomatillos, tomatoes and ¼ cup cilantro in a food processor until almost smooth.

Heat the olive oil in a large Dutch oven or heavy pan. Sauté the onion in the oil for 5 to 7 minutes or until tender. Add the jalapeño, Anaheim pepper, garlic and cumin. Sauté for 3 minutes or until fragrant and the peppers are tender. Stir in the tomatillo purée, chicken and broth. Simmer, partially covered, for 20 minutes. Season with salt and pepper. Ladle into soup bowls. Chop the remaining cilantro to taste. Sprinkle over the soup. Add chili oil, tortilla chips and sour cream.

Corn and Wild Rice Soup with Smoked Sausage

SERVES 12

12½ cups low-sodium chicken broth, divided
1¼ cups wild rice (about 8½ ounces)
6¼ cups frozen corn kernels (about 2½ pounds), thawed, divided

2 tablespoons vegetable oil
10 ounces fully cooked smoked sausage (such as kielbasa), cut into ½-inch cubes
3 carrots, peeled and chopped

2 medium onions, chopped
1½ cups half-and-half
Salt and pepper to taste
Chopped fresh chives to taste
Chopped fresh parsley to taste

Bring 5 cups of the broth to a simmer in a medium heavy saucepan over medium heat. Add the rice. Simmer for 40 minutes or until the rice is almost tender and all of the liquid is absorbed, stirring occasionally. Process 3¾ cups of the corn kernels and 1½ cups of the broth in a food processor just until puréed.

Heat the vegetable oil in a large heavy Dutch oven over medium-high heat. Sauté the sausage in the oil for 5 minutes or until brown. Add the carrots and onions. Cook for 3 minutes, stirring frequently. Add the remaining 6 cups broth. Bring to a simmer. Add the rice, puréed corn and remaining 2½ cups corn kernels. Cook for 15 minutes or until the flavors are blended and the rice is very tender. Stir in the half-and-half. Add additional broth if desired. Season with salt and pepper. Ladle into soup bowls. Sprinkle with chives and parsley.

DISCOVER DENVER

Washington Park, located south of downtown Denver, is a 155-acre green space surrounded by a bustling urban neighborhood of the same name. The park has two lakes, two formal flower gardens (one of which is an exact replica of George Washington's garden at Mt. Vernon), sports courts, and miles of pathways. "Wash Park" is a great place to play, run, walk, or boat in the heart of metro Denver!

Italian Sausage and Tortellini Soup

SERVES 8

8 ounces ground hot Italian sausage
8 ounces ground mild Italian sausage
1 cup chopped onion
2 cloves garlic, sliced
6 cups beef broth
2 cups water
½ cup dry red wine
1 (14-ounce) can diced tomatoes,
   drained

1 (14-ounce) can tomato sauce
1 cup thinly sliced carrots
½ teaspoon dried basil
½ teaspoon dried oregano
1½ cups sliced zucchini
8 ounces cheese tortellini
3 tablespoons chopped fresh parsley

Brown the hot Italian sausage and mild Italian sausage in a Dutch oven, stirring to crumble. Remove to a plate, reserving 1 tablespoon of the drippings in the pan. Sauté the onion and garlic in the reserved drippings until tender. Add the sausage, broth, water, wine, tomatoes, tomato sauce, carrots, basil and oregano. Bring to a boil. Simmer over medium-low heat for 30 minutes. Skim off and discard any fat. Stir in the zucchini, tortellini and parsley. Simmer for 35 to 40 minutes.

Entertaining Tip

Celebrate crisp nights with these cozy ideas: Simple lanterns are a stylish option to light the way. Instead of flowers, opt for potted plants or trees to anchor your serving area. Add a toasty fire to set the stage for a magical (and warm) gathering. Serve soup in hollowed-out loaves of bread—not only are they tasty, but also they make cleanup easier! Set out warm blankets in pretty baskets for a cozy vibe. Use vintage insulated bottles to keep soups and drinks hot.

Slow Cooker Bison Chili

SERVES 10

1 pound ground bison
1 pound ground hot Italian pork
    sausage
1 large onion, chopped
3 to 5 medium jalapeños or poblano
    peppers, seeded and chopped

3 cloves garlic, minced
2 (15-ounce) cans black beans,
    drained
2 (14-ounce) cans fire-roasted
    diced tomatoes
1 (28-ounce) can crushed tomatoes

2 teaspoons ancho chili powder
Cajun or Creole seasoning to taste
Hot sauce to taste
Salt and pepper to taste
Shredded sharp white Cheddar
    cheese

Brown the ground bison and pork sausage in a large pan, stirring to crumble; drain, reserving half the drippings in the pan. Combine the bison mixture and reserved drippings in a slow cooker. Add the onion, jalapeños, garlic, beans, undrained diced tomatoes, crushed tomatoes and chili powder and mix well. Season with Cajun seasoning, hot sauce, salt and pepper. Cook, covered, on Low for 10 to 12 hours. Ladle into soup bowls. Sprinkle with Cheddar cheese.

White Bean and Swiss Chard Soup

SERVES 4 TO 6

2 tablespoons extra-virgin olive oil
2 medium onions, chopped
2 ribs celery, chopped
2 medium carrots, chopped
3 cloves garlic, minced
1 tablespoon chopped fresh
    rosemary leaves

1 tablespoon chopped fresh
    thyme leaves
½ teaspoon red pepper flakes
1 bay leaf
3 (15-ounce) cans cannellini beans,
    rinsed and drained
4 cups vegetable stock

Parmesan cheese rind
1 bunch Swiss chard, stemmed
    and cut into bite-size pieces
1 teaspoon balsamic vinegar
Salt and pepper to taste
Grated fresh Parmesan cheese

Heat the olive oil in a large pot over medium-high heat. Cook the onions, celery and carrots in the oil for 5 minutes or until tender and the onion is translucent. Add the garlic. Sauté for 1 minute or until fragrant. Add the rosemary, thyme, red pepper flakes and bay leaf. Stir in the beans. Cook for 1 to 2 minutes or until heated through. Add the stock and Parmesan cheese rind. Bring to a boil. Simmer, partially covered, over low heat for 30 minutes or until thickened, stirring occasionally. Add the Swiss chard. Cook for 3 minutes or until wilted, stirring occasionally. Stir in the vinegar, salt and pepper. Remove and discard the Parmesan cheese rind and bay leaf. Ladle into soup bowls and sprinkle with grated Parmesan cheese. Serve with warm crusty bread.

SLOW COOKER BISON CHILI

Portobello Mushroom Chowder

SERVES 4 TO 6

4 tablespoons butter
1½ pounds potatoes, peeled and
    finely chopped
1 pound portobello mushrooms,
    sliced and cut into bite-size pieces

2 cups chopped carrots
1 cup chopped celery
½ cup chopped onion
¼ cup all-purpose flour
1½ teaspoons ground black pepper

2 cups beef broth
1 cup half-and-half
Salt to taste
2 tablespoons chopped
    Italian parsley

Melt the butter in a large heavy soup pot over medium-high heat. Sauté the potatoes, mushrooms, carrots, celery and onion in the butter for 15 minutes or until tender. Stir in the flour and pepper. Cook for 1 minute, stirring constantly. Add the broth gradually, stirring constantly. Bring to a boil. Simmer over medium-low heat for 20 to 30 minutes or until the flavors marry. Add the half-and-half. Cook until heated through; do not boil. Season with salt. Stir in the parsley. Ladle into soup bowls and serve.

Sweet Potato Soup

SERVES 4 TO 6

1 tablespoon extra-virgin
    avocado or olive oil
1 medium yellow onion, coarsely
    chopped
½ cup chopped celery
½ cup chopped red bell pepper
3 cloves garlic, minced

8 cups peeled coarsely chopped
    sweet potatoes
4 cups low-sodium vegetable broth
2 (13-ounce) cans light coconut milk
2 teaspoons ground cinnamon
1 teaspoon ground black pepper
1 teaspoon sea salt

½ teaspoon crushed red pepper flakes
½ teaspoon dried thyme
½ teaspoon paprika
1 tablespoon pure maple syrup
1 teaspoon pure vanilla extract
2 tablespoons chopped fresh
    Italian parsley

Heat a large stockpot or Dutch oven over medium-high heat. Add the avocado oil, onion, celery and bell pepper. Cook for 5 to 7 minutes or until tender, stirring frequently. Add the garlic. Cook for 30 seconds, stirring constantly. Add the sweet potatoes, broth, coconut milk, cinnamon, black pepper, salt, red pepper flakes, thyme and paprika in order, stirring after each addition. Bring to a gentle boil over high heat. Simmer, partially covered, over medium-low heat for 15 minutes or until the sweet potatoes are fork tender. Stir in the maple syrup and vanilla extract. Turn off the stove. Let the soup stand for 5 minutes. Process the soup with an immersion blender or in half-full batches in a blender on low speed until the desired consistency is reached. Ladle into soup bowls. Sprinkle with equal portions of the parsley.

Chilled Roasted Tomato Soup

SERVES 4 TO 6

2 pounds large red tomatoes
1 large red bell pepper
1 medium cucumber, peeled, seeded
 and coarsely chopped
3 small green onions, chopped (white
 bulbs only)

1 clove garlic
2 (5-ounce) cans tomato juice, divided
2 tablespoons red wine vinegar
Salt and pepper to taste
Basil pesto to taste
Extra-virgin olive oil to taste

Preheat the oven to 400 degrees or the grill to medium.

Roast the tomatoes and bell pepper on a baking sheet or grill on the grill rack until charred. Let the tomatoes stand to cool. Place the bell pepper in a plastic or paper bag. Let stand to cool. Peel and core the tomatoes. Peel, core and seed the bell pepper.

Process the tomatoes, bell pepper, cucumber, green onions, garlic and ½ cup of the tomato juice in a food processor until smooth. Pour into a large bowl. Stir in the remaining tomato juice and vinegar. Chill, covered, for 2 to 24 hours. Season with salt and pepper. Ladle into soup bowls or mugs. Top with basil pesto and olive oil.

Founded in 1986, The Gathering Place is the only daytime drop-in center in metropolitan Denver that serves women, their children, and transgender individuals who are experiencing poverty or homelessness. Since 2010, the Junior League of Denver has partnered with The Gathering Place to expand and improve their current nutrition program. In addition to providing a year's worth of milk, League volunteers prepare and serve two meals a month.

Slow Cooker Tomato and Carrot Soup

SERVES 4

2 pounds Roma tomatoes, cut into
    quarters
1 medium yellow onion, cut into
    ¼-inch slices
4 medium carrots, cut into
    ½-inch slices

¼ cup extra-virgin olive oil
2 teaspoons salt
Freshly ground pepper to taste
2 cups low-sodium chicken or
    vegetable broth
3 cloves garlic, minced

½ teaspoon paprika
¼ teaspoon cayenne pepper
¼ cup heavy cream

Preheat the oven to 425 degrees. Line a rimmed baking sheet with foil and spray the foil with nonstick cooking spray, or use a nonstick baking sheet.

Combine the tomatoes, onion and carrots in a large bowl. Add the olive oil, salt and pepper and toss to coat. Spread on the prepared baking sheet. Roast for 25 minutes or until tender and just beginning to brown, stirring occasionally.

Place the tomato mixture and any juices in a slow cooker. Add the broth, garlic, paprika and cayenne pepper and mix well. Cook on Low for 6 to 8 hours. Turn off the slow cooker and let stand to cool for 5 minutes. Stir in the cream. Process the soup in batches in a blender or with an immersion blender until smooth. Return to the slow cooker. Ladle into soup bowls.

DISCOVER DENVER

"Love this City" mural by Pat Milbery, located at Broadway and Arapahoe Street

Classic Chicken Salad Sandwiches

SERVES 25

1 quart chicken broth
1 rib celery with leaves
1 medium carrot
1 medium onion, cut into halves
2 teaspoons ground black pepper

⅜ teaspoon ground cayenne
  pepper, divided
8 chicken breast halves
1½ cups finely chopped celery
1 to 2 cups mayonnaise,
  divided

2 tablespoons lemon juice
Salt to taste
4 eggs, hard-boiled, peeled and grated
½ cup butter, softened
2 loaves sandwich bread, end pieces
  discarded and crusts removed

Combine the broth, 1 rib celery with leaves, carrot, onion, black pepper and ⅛ teaspoon of the cayenne pepper in a large pot. Bring to a boil. Add the chicken. Return to a boil. Cook, covered, over medium-low heat until the chicken is cooked through. Let the chicken cool in the broth. Remove the chicken and chop finely, removing and discarding any skin and bones.

Combine the chicken, chopped celery, 1 cup of the mayonnaise, lemon juice, remaining ¼ teaspoon cayenne pepper and salt to taste in a large bowl and mix well. Fold in the eggs. Stir in spoonfuls of the remaining mayonnaise until the desired consistency is reached. Chill, covered, overnight.

Spread a thin layer of the butter over one side of each slice of bread. Spread equal portions of the chicken salad over the buttered side of half the bread. Place the remaining half of the bread buttered side down on the chicken salad. Cut into 4 triangles or squares with an electric knife if possible. Arrange on a platter in 2 layers. Cover with plastic wrap. Place a damp paper towel on top and cover with additional plastic wrap; the paper towel keeps the sandwiches moist. Serve chilled.

Cucumber Tea Sandwiches

SERVES 10 TO 12

1 large English cucumber
8 ounces cream cheese, softened
⅓ cup chopped fresh dill

2 teaspoons fresh lemon juice
1 teaspoon grated lemon zest
¼ teaspoon salt

4 tablespoons butter, softened
1 loaf sandwich bread, end pieces
  discarded and crusts removed

Cut the cucumber into thin slices with a mandoline if possible. Arrange on paper towels to drain. Combine the cream cheese, dill, lemon juice, lemon zest and salt in a large bowl and mix until smooth. Spread a thin layer of the butter over one side of each slice of bread. Spread a thin layer of the cream cheese mixture over half the bread slices. Add a layer of cucumber slices. Place the remaining half of the bread buttered side down on the cucumbers. Cut into 4 squares, 3 rectangles or 4 triangles with an electric knife if possible. May use a combination of white and wheat bread. Garnish with sprigs of fresh dill.

Beer-Braised Short Rib Sliders

SERVES 12

2½ to 3 pounds boneless beef
   short ribs
Salt and pepper to taste
2 tablespoons extra-virgin olive oil
12 ounces Mexican lager-style beer
½ medium yellow onion, chopped

2 cloves garlic, minced
1 (14-ounce) can fire-roasted diced
   tomatoes
¼ cup beef broth
1 tablespoon rice wine vinegar
1 tablespoon brown sugar

1 teaspoon ancho chili powder
½ teaspoon paprika
12 slider buns or Hawaiian dinner rolls
Roasted Poblano Slaw (recipe below)
1 cup crumbled queso fresco

Preheat the oven to 350 degrees. Trim the short ribs if needed; pat dry. Season generously with salt and pepper.

Heat the olive oil in a large oven-safe lidded pan or Dutch oven over medium-high to high heat. Brown the short ribs on all sides in the oil. Remove to a plate, reserving the pan drippings. Remove the pan from the heat.

Add the beer, stirring to deglaze the pan. Add the onion, garlic, tomatoes, broth, vinegar, brown sugar, chili powder and paprika and mix well. Season with salt and pepper. Return the short ribs to the pan. Bring the liquid to a boil. Remove from the heat. Bake, covered, for 2½ hours or until the short ribs are very tender.

Shred the short ribs. Cut the rolls horizontally into halves, arranging cut sides up on a baking sheet. Broil for 2 or 3 minutes or until golden brown. Spoon equal portions of the short ribs, Roasted Poblano Slaw and queso fresco onto the bottom of each roll. Place the tops of the rolls on the sliders.

ROASTED POBLANO SLAW

1 medium poblano pepper
2 tablespoons honey
2 tablespoons extra-virgin olive oil
2 tablespoons lime juice

2 tablespoons rice vinegar
4 cups shredded cabbage
½ cup chopped cilantro
Salt and pepper to taste

Preheat the broiler to high. Line a baking sheet with foil. Spray the foil with nonstick cooking spray.

Place the poblano pepper on the prepared baking sheet. Roast until brown, turning once. Let stand to cool. Remove the charred peeling using the backside of a sharp knife. Remove and discard the seeds. Cut into 1-inch-long thin strips.

Whisk the honey, olive oil, lime juice and vinegar in a small bowl until well blended. Combine the cabbage, poblano pepper and cilantro in a bowl and mix well. Pour the honey mixture over the cabbage mixture and stir to coat. Season with salt and pepper. Chill, covered, until serving time.

Mediterranean Pita Sandwiches

SERVES 4

½ cup crumbled feta cheese
⅓ cup plus 2 tablespoons steak
  sauce, divided
2 tablespoons chopped
  kalamata olives
2 tablespoons mayonnaise

1 pound ground beef
4 medium pita breads, split
Diced tomatoes
Diced red onion
4 romaine lettuce leaves

Combine the feta cheese, 2 tablespoons of the steak sauce, olives and mayonnaise in a bowl and mix well. Chill, covered, for 1 hour or longer. Combine the ground beef and the remaining ⅓ cup of the steak sauce in a bowl and mix well. Shape into 4 patties, arranging on a plate. Chill for 30 minutes.

Preheat the grill or a large sauté pan to medium.

Cook the patties for 4 minutes per side for medium-rare or to the desired doneness. Place a hamburger patty in each pita bread. Add tomatoes, onion, lettuce and equal portions of the feta cheese mixture. Serve immediately.

DISCOVER DENVER

The Highlands neighborhood in West Denver is full of trendy restaurants and bars, historical craftsman homes, mature parks, and an eclectic mix of urbanites. Rooftop patios are popular, as many buildings have incredible views of downtown. The Highlands is home to multiple craft breweries, coffee shops, ice cream shops, and street fairs. The Highlands also hosts the Colorado Dragon Boat Festival. Held each summer, the festival features delicious Asian food and artwork, and competitors race colorful dragon boats across Sloan's Lake.

ROASTED VEGETABLE AND GOURNAY GRILLED CHEESE SANDWICHES

Roasted Vegetable and Gournay Grilled Cheese Sandwiches

SERVES 4 TO 8

3 medium zucchini
1 medium red bell pepper
1 medium red onion
3 tablespoons extra-virgin olive oil
Salt and pepper to taste

8 ounces Gournay cheese with garlic
  and fine herbs (such as Boursin®)
8 slices sourdough bread
4 tablespoons butter, softened
8 slices Havarti cheese

Preheat the oven to 450 degrees. Spray a baking pan with nonstick cooking spray or use a nonstick baking pan.

Cut the zucchini diagonally into ¼-inch slices. Cut the bell pepper and onion into ¼-inch slices. Combine the zucchini, bell pepper, onion and olive oil in a large bowl and toss to coat. Season with salt and pepper. Spread in the prepared baking pan. Roast for 20 minutes or until tender and beginning to brown.

Spread 1 ounce of the Gournay cheese over each slice of bread. Spread 1 teaspoon of the butter on the other side of each slice. Layer a slice of Havarti cheese, a fourth of the roasted vegetables and a slice of Havarti cheese on the Gournay cheese side of each of 4 slices of bread. Place a slice of the remaining bread Gournay cheese side down on top of each sandwich. Grill over medium heat in a nonstick pan or in a panini press until the cheese is melted and the sandwiches are golden brown and crisp, turning once if in a nonstick pan. Cut into halves if desired.

Grilled Fig, Brie and Arugula Sandwiches with Honey Drizzle

SERVES 4

1 loaf ciabatta bread
8 ounces Brie cheese, thinly sliced
Extra-virgin olive oil
5 ounces arugula

6 ounces thinly sliced prosciutto
8 tablespoons fig spread
Honey to taste

Heat the grill or pan to medium. Cut the bread into eight ½- to ¾-inch slices. Brush one side of each slice lightly with olive oil. Place oiled side down on the grill. Grill for 30 seconds. Brush the uncooked sides of the slices with olive oil. Place uncooked sides down on the grill. Spread each slice with 1 tablespoon of the fig spread. Layer each with 3 slices of the Brie cheese, a small handful of arugula and 3 slices of the prosciutto. Grill for 2 minutes or just until the Brie cheese begins to melt and light grill marks appear on the bread. Remove 2 open-faced sandwiches to each of 4 plates. Drizzle each with honey. Close to make sandwiches or serve open-faced.

Desserts

Menu

Home for the Holidays

Cranberry and Pomegranate Bruschetta ~ 23

Pesto Cheesecake ~ 39

Roast Beef Tenderloins
with Shallot Confit and Wine Sauce ~ 152

Roasted Broccoli and Green Beans
with Asiago Cheese ~ 204

Potato Gratin with Gournay Cheese ~ 218

Chocolate Pavlova ~ 273

Gingerbread Cookie Edible Ornaments ~ 278

Shopping for a Cause

Every fall, shoppers gather for the Junior League of Denver's annual Mile High Holiday Mart. Since the first League-sponsored "Christmas Mart" in 1980, this event has helped raise more than $6 million in support of League projects in the Denver community. It is not only one of the most popular holiday shopping events in the area, but also one of the League's longest-running and most successful fundraisers.

Buttermilk Cake with Strawberry, Rhubarb and Lemon Sauce

SERVES 6 TO 8

1 cup buttermilk
½ cup butter, melted
3 eggs
1 to 1½ cups sugar

½ cup baking mix (such as Bisquik™)
1 teaspoon vanilla extract
Strawberry, Rhubarb and Lemon
    Sauce (recipe below)

Preheat the oven to 350 degrees. Grease a 9-inch metal pie plate.

Combine the buttermilk, butter, eggs, sugar, baking mix and vanilla extract in a blender. Process on high for 30 seconds or until blended. Pour into the prepared pie plate. Bake for 35 to 40 minutes or until set and the cake is pulling away from the side. Let stand to cool completely. Cut into slices. Top servings with Strawberry, Rhubarb and Lemon Sauce.

STRAWBERRY, RHUBARB AND LEMON SAUCE

2 cups rhubarb slices (¼ inch)
2 cups strawberry slices (¼ to ½ inch)
1½ cups water
½ cup sugar
Juice and grated zest of 1 lemon

Combine the rhubarb, strawberries, water, sugar and lemon juice in a medium saucepan. Bring to a boil. Simmer over medium to medium-low heat for 20 minutes or until the fruit is cooked down and the sauce is reduced slightly. Stir in the lemon zest. Let stand to cool for 5 minutes. Process in a blender or food processor until smooth.

DISCOVER DENVER

"Larimer Boy and Girl" mural by Jeremy Burns, located at 27th Street and Larimer Street

Tres Leches Cake

SERVES 10 TO 12

1½ cups all-purpose flour
1 tablespoon baking powder
4 eggs, separated
½ cup sugar
½ cup whole milk

1 (14-ounce) can sweetened
   condensed milk
1 (12-ounce) can evaporated milk
3 cups heavy whipping cream,
   divided

¼ cup orange liqueur
2 tablespoons powdered sugar
½ teaspoon ground cinnamon
   (optional)

Preheat the oven to 350 degrees. Grease and flour a 9×13-inch glass baking dish. Sift the flour and baking powder into a small bowl.

Whisk the egg whites in a large mixing bowl until frothy. Add the sugar 1 tablespoon at a time, beating constantly at medium-high speed. Beat until stiff peaks form. Add the egg yolks one at a time, beating well after each addition. Add the flour mixture ½ cup at a time alternately with the whole milk ¼ cup at a time, beating constantly. Beat until smooth, scraping the side of the bowl as needed. Spoon into the prepared baking dish. Bake for 25 to 30 minutes or until a wooden pick inserted near the center comes out clean; the cake should be brown and spring back when pressed. Let stand to cool for 10 minutes.

Whisk the sweetened condensed milk, evaporated milk, 1 cup of the whipping cream and orange liqueur in a bowl until blended. Pierce the cake all over with a skewer or large fork. Pour the milk sauce evenly over the cake, allowing the sauce to soak into the cake. Let stand to cool completely. Chill for 3 hours or longer.

Combine the remaining 2 cups whipping cream and powdered sugar in a large mixing bowl. Beat until soft peaks form. Spread over the cake. Sprinkle with the cinnamon. Chill until serving time.

Carrot Cake with Lemon Frosting

SERVES 8 TO 10

1 pound carrots, peeled and
   cut into ½-inch pieces
1½ cups vegetable oil
1 (8-ounce) can crushed pineapple,
   drained

4 eggs
1 tablespoon vanilla extract
3 cups unbleached all-purpose flour
2½ cups sugar
1 tablespoon ground cinnamon

1 tablespoon baking soda
1 teaspoon salt
1½ cups coarsely chopped walnuts
   (about 6 ounces)
Lemon Frosting (recipe below)

Combine the carrots and enough salted water to cover in a large pot. Bring to a boil. Boil for 12 minutes or until tender; drain. Purée the carrots in a food processor, scraping the side of the bowl occasionally. Spoon into a large bowl. Let stand to cool.

Preheat the oven to 350 degrees. Butter three 9-inch round cake pans and line with parchment paper.

Whisk the vegetable oil, pineapple, eggs and vanilla extract into the carrots. Combine the flour, sugar, cinnamon, baking soda and salt in a medium bowl and mix well. Stir into the carrot mixture. Fold in the walnuts. Divide the batter evenly among the prepared cake pans. Bake for 35 minutes or until a cake tester inserted near the centers comes out clean. Cool in the pans on wire racks.

Spread the Lemon Frosting between the layers and over the top and side of the cake, using ¾ cup of frosting each for the first two layers and the remaining frosting for the top. May be made a day ahead; chill, covered with a cake dome. Let stand at room temperature for 3 hours before serving.

LEMON FROSTING

1 pound cream cheese, softened
1¼ cups unsalted butter, softened
1 tablespoon fresh lemon juice

2 teaspoons vanilla extract
5¾ cups powdered sugar, sifted

Combine the cream cheese, butter, lemon juice and vanilla extract in a mixing bowl. Beat until light and fluffy. Add the powdered sugar gradually, beating constantly. Chill for 1 hour or until firm but spreadable.

Carrot Coconut Cupcakes

MAKES 24

1 cup sugar
½ cup vegetable oil
2 eggs
1 cup all-purpose flour
1 teaspoon baking soda

1 teaspoon ground cinnamon
½ teaspoon salt
¼ teaspoon ground nutmeg
2 (8-ounce) cans crushed pineapple,
    drained

1 cup peeled and grated carrots
¾ cup sweetened flaked coconut
¼ cup chopped pecans
White Chocolate Frosting
    (recipe below)

Preheat the oven to 350 degrees. Line 24 muffin cups with paper liners.

Whisk the sugar, vegetable oil and eggs in a large bowl until blended. Whisk the flour, baking soda, cinnamon, salt and nutmeg in a medium bowl. Combine the pineapple, carrots, coconut and pecans in a medium bowl and mix well. Stir the flour mixture into the sugar mixture. Fold in the pineapple mixture. Divide the batter evenly among the prepared muffin cups. Bake for 20 minutes or until golden brown and a cake tester inserted near the centers comes out clean. Remove the cupcakes to a wire rack. Let stand to cool completely. Spread the White Chocolate Frosting over the cupcakes. Chill, covered, until serving time.

WHITE CHOCOLATE FROSTING

1½ ounces white chocolate, chopped
    (about ¼ cup)
8 ounces cream cheese, softened

4 tablespoons unsalted butter,
    softened
1 cup powdered sugar

Melt the white chocolate in the top of a double boiler over barely simmering water, stirring until smooth. Spoon into a food processor. Add the cream cheese and butter and pulse until blended. Add the powdered sugar and process until smooth.

Denver Chocolate Sheet Cake

Favorite recipe from Colorado Cache chosen by Chairman Jaydee Boat

SERVES 12 TO 16

2 ⅓ cups all-purpose flour
2 cups sugar
1 teaspoon baking soda
1 cup butter
1 ¼ cups water

4 tablespoons baking cocoa
½ cup buttermilk
2 eggs, beaten
1 teaspoon vanilla extract
Chocolate Frosting (recipe below)

Preheat the oven to 350 degrees. Grease a 9×13-inch baking pan.

Combine the flour, sugar and baking soda in a bowl and mix well. Combine the butter, water and baking cocoa in a saucepan. Bring to a boil, stirring frequently. Add to the flour mixture and mix well. Add the buttermilk, eggs and vanilla extract and mix well. Spoon into the prepared baking pan. Bake for 30 minutes or until the cake tests done. Spread with the warm Chocolate Frosting; the frosting will harden as it cools.

CHOCOLATE FROSTING

½ cup butter
6 tablespoons buttermilk
4 tablespoons baking cocoa

1 teaspoon vanilla extract
16 ounces powdered sugar
½ cup chopped walnuts or pecans

Combine the butter, buttermilk and baking cocoa in a saucepan. Bring to a boil, stirring frequently. Remove from the heat. Stir in the vanilla extract. Add the powdered sugar and mix well. Fold in the walnuts.

First published in 1978, *Colorado Cache* was the first cookbook from the Junior League of Denver. This treasure trove of recipes reflects Colorado's casual style of living, rich heritage, and natural bounty.

"I am often asked (still!) how we acquired so many great recipes— and it was the determination of the testers to find the best."

—*Jaydee Boat*

Candied Ginger Cake with Toffee Sauce

SERVES 8

2 cups Medjool dates, chopped
1 teaspoon baking soda
1 cup boiling water
2 cups all-purpose flour
2 teaspoons baking powder

½ teaspoon kosher salt
½ cup unsalted butter, softened
1 cup packed dark brown sugar
2 teaspoons finely grated fresh ginger
3 eggs

⅓ cup chopped crystallized ginger
Toffee Sauce (recipe below)
Demerara sugar

Preheat the oven to 350 degrees. Grease and flour a 9-cup bundt pan, covering completely.

Combine the dates and baking soda in a small heatproof bowl and toss to coat. Add the water. Let stand for 10 to 15 minutes or until the dates are very tender. Mash lightly with a fork; mixture will be thick but not smooth.

Whisk the flour, baking powder and salt in a medium bowl. Beat the butter, brown sugar and fresh ginger in a large mixing bowl for 4 minutes or until light and fluffy. Add the eggs one at a time, beating well after each addition. Add the flour mixture alternately with the date mixture half at a time, beating constantly. Fold in the crystallized ginger.

Spoon into the prepared pan. Bake for 35 to 45 minutes or until the top springs back when lightly pressed and a cake tester inserted near the center comes out clean. Place the pan on a wire rack inside a rimmed baking sheet. Let stand to cool for 10 minutes. Invert onto the wire rack; wipe out the bundt pan. Let stand to cool for 20 minutes; cake will be warm.

Pierce the warm cake all over with a wooden pick. Pour a third of the Toffee Sauce evenly into the bundt pan. Return the cake to the pan carefully. Poke holes over the bottom of the cake. Pour a portion of the remaining Toffee Sauce over the cake. Let stand for 15 to 20 minutes or until the sauce is absorbed into the cake.

Invert onto the wire rack. Sprinkle with Demerara sugar. Reheat the remaining Toffee Sauce and serve with the cake. Store, tightly covered, at room temperature until serving time.

TOFFEE SAUCE

1 cup packed dark brown sugar
1 cup heavy cream
¾ cup unsalted butter

2 tablespoons water
1 teaspoon kosher salt

Combine the brown sugar, cream, butter, water and salt in a small saucepan. Bring to a boil over medium-low heat, stirring frequently. Cook for 5 to 8 minutes or until the mixture coats the back of a spoon, stirring constantly. Let stand to cool slightly.

Orange Olive Oil Cupcakes

MAKES 12

1½ cups all-purpose flour
1¼ teaspoons baking powder
¼ teaspoon salt
1 cup sugar
½ cup extra-virgin olive oil
2 eggs, at room temperature

2 teaspoons grated orange zest
2 teaspoons vanilla extract
⅔ cup whole milk, at room
  temperature
Marmalade Frosting (recipe below)

Preheat the oven to 350 degrees. Line 12 muffin cups with paper liners.

Mix the flour, baking powder and salt in a small bowl. Beat the sugar and olive oil in a mixing bowl using the paddle attachment on medium speed for 1 to 2 minutes or until blended. Add the eggs one at a time, beating just until incorporated after each addition. Beat in the orange zest and vanilla extract. Beat in half the flour mixture at medium-low speed. Beat in the milk and remaining flour mixture. Fill the prepared muffin cups two-thirds full with the batter. Bake for 14 to 16 minutes or until the tops spring back when lightly pressed. Let stand to cool for 5 minutes. Remove the cupcakes to a wire rack to cool completely. Spread with the Marmalade Frosting. Garnish with orange peel curls.

MARMALADE FROSTING

½ cup orange marmalade
1 cup unsalted butter, softened
2 cups powdered sugar, sifted
½ teaspoon vanilla extract
⅛ teaspoon salt

Process the orange marmalade in a food processor until finely chopped. Cream the butter in a mixing bowl using the paddle attachment for 30 seconds or until pale and smooth, increasing the speed from low to medium-high gradually. Beat in the powdered sugar ½ cup at a time, scraping the side of the bowl as needed. Add the orange marmalade, vanilla extract and salt. Beat at low speed until blended. Whip at medium-high to high speed for 3 to 4 minutes or until smooth and creamy, scraping the side of the bowl occasionally.

Peach Cupcakes with Brown Sugar Frosting

MAKES 24

3 cups plus 1 tablespoon
   cake flour, divided
1½ teaspoons baking soda
1 teaspoon baking powder
1 teaspoon kosher salt

¼ teaspoon freshly grated or
   ground nutmeg
¾ cup unsalted butter, softened
¾ cup packed light brown sugar
½ cup granulated sugar
2 eggs

1½ cups sour cream
½ teaspoon vanilla extract
2 to 2¼ cups chopped fresh or
   thawed frozen peaches
Brown Sugar Frosting (recipe below)

Preheat the oven to 350 degrees. Line 24 muffin cups with paper liners.

Sift 3 cups of the flour, baking soda, baking powder, salt and nutmeg into a large bowl. Beat the butter, brown sugar and granulated sugar in a mixing bowl for at least 2 minutes or until light and fluffy. Scrape the side of the bowl. Add the eggs one at a time, beating constantly for at least 2 minutes and scraping the side of the bowl after each addition. Beat in the sour cream and vanilla extract. Stir in the flour mixture. Pat the peaches dry with a paper towel. Toss the peaches with the remaining 1 tablespoon flour and fold into the batter. Fill the prepared muffin cups two-thirds full with the batter. Bake for 18 to 20 minutes or until a cake tester inserted near the centers comes out clean. Let stand to cool for 10 minutes. Remove the cupcakes to a wire rack to cool completely. May be frozen for up to 1 week before frosting. Spread with the Brown Sugar Frosting. Garnish with small peach slices and sprinkle with cinnamon.

BROWN SUGAR FROSTING

2 cups unsalted butter, softened
1 cup packed brown sugar
2 teaspoons ground cinnamon
1 teaspoon vanilla extract
¼ teaspoon salt
3 cups powdered sugar

Cream the butter and brown sugar in a mixing bowl until light and fluffy. Beat in the cinnamon, vanilla extract and salt. Add the powdered sugar ½ cup at a time, beating well after each addition and scraping the bowl as needed. Beat at medium speed for 2 to 3 minutes or until light and fluffy, scraping the bowl frequently.

Hummingbird Cake with Cream Cheese Icing

SERVES 8 TO 10

---

3 cups all-purpose flour
2 cups sugar
1 teaspoon baking soda
1 teaspoon salt
1 teaspoon ground cinnamon
1 (8-ounce) can crushed pineapple

3 ripe medium bananas, mashed
1 cup chopped pecans, toasted
1 cup vegetable oil
3 eggs, beaten
2 teaspoons vanilla extract
Cream Cheese Icing (recipe below)

Preheat the oven to 350 degrees. Grease 3 round 9-inch cake pans.

Whisk or sift the flour, sugar, baking soda, salt and cinnamon in a large bowl. Combine the undrained pineapple, bananas, pecans, vegetable oil, eggs and vanilla extract in a medium bowl and mix well. Add to the flour mixture and stir just until mixed; do not overmix. Divide the batter evenly among the prepared cake pans. Bake for 30 minutes or until a wooden pick inserted near the center comes out clean. Remove to wire racks to cool completely. Spread the Cream Cheese Icing between the layers and over the top and side of the cake. Garnish with edible flowers.

CREAM CHEESE ICING

---

16 ounces cream cheese, softened
1 cup butter, softened

1 teaspoon vanilla extract
32 ounces powdered sugar

Beat the cream cheese and butter in a mixing bowl until blended. Beat in the vanilla extract. Add the powdered sugar 1 cup at a time, beating constantly at low speed and scraping the side of the bowl occasionally.

Tomato Soup Spice Cake

SERVES 12

2 cups all-purpose flour
2 teaspoons baking powder
1 teaspoon baking soda
¼ teaspoon salt
2 teaspoons ground cinnamon
1 teaspoon ground cloves

2 cups sugar
1 tablespoon shortening
2 medium eggs
2 (10-ounce) cans condensed
  tomato soup
Cream Cheese Frosting (recipe below)

Preheat the oven to 375 degrees. Grease and flour a 9×13-inch baking pan.

Combine the flour, baking powder, baking soda, salt, cinnamon and cloves in a bowl and mix well. Beat the sugar, shortening and eggs in a mixing bowl. Beat in the tomato soup. Add the flour mixture and mix well. Spoon into the prepared baking pan. Bake for 40 minutes or until a wooden pick inserted near the center comes out clean. Let stand to cool. Spread with the Cream Cheese Frosting.

CREAM CHEESE FROSTING

8 ounces cream cheese, softened
1 teaspoon pure vanilla extract
2½ cups powdered sugar

Beat the cream cheese and vanilla extract in a mixing bowl. Add the powdered sugar gradually, beating until blended after each addition.

It is believed that the first recipes for tomato soup cake originated in the late 1920s or early 1930s as a way to use creative and inexpensive ingredients to recreate family favorites for less. The Junior League of Denver also had to learn to do more with less during this time. In 1929–1930, JLD raised money by collecting and selling tinfoil. Members distributed 350 cardboard boxes labeled "Save Tinfoil for the Junior League" throughout the city. Driving a truck for collection, members brought in 434 pounds during the first six weeks and sold them for five cents a pound.

Black-Bottom Banana Cream Pie

SERVES 8

2 (5-ounce) packages all-butter
  shortbread cookies
¼ teaspoon salt, divided
3 tablespoons unsalted butter, melted
2 cups whole milk
½ cup sugar

¼ cup cornstarch
4 egg yolks
3 ounces bittersweet chocolate
  (60 to 70 percent cacao), divided
1 cup plus 1 tablespoon cold heavy
  cream, divided

3 teaspoons pure vanilla extract,
  divided
2 tablespoons unsalted cold butter
2 large ripe bananas
1 tablespoon powdered sugar
Slivered almonds (optional)

Pulse the cookies and ⅛ teaspoon of the salt in a food processor until finely ground and beginning to stick to the side; may crush the cookies into fine crumbs in a sealable plastic bag. Add the melted butter and pulse or stir just until incorporated. Press evenly over the bottom and side of a 9-inch pie plate. Freeze the pie shell.

Whisk the milk, sugar, cornstarch and remaining ⅛ teaspoon salt in a heavy saucepan until blended. Whisk in the egg yolks. Cook over medium-high heat for 5 minutes or until the custard boils and is very thick. Remove from the heat. Place 2 ounces of the chocolate in a small heatproof bowl. Add ½ cup of the custard. Let stand for 1 minute to allow the chocolate to melt. Stir in 1 tablespoon of the cream and 1 teaspoon of the vanilla extract. Spread over the bottom of the prepared pie shell. Chill for 2 hours or until firm.

Meanwhile, whisk the cold butter into the hot custard in the saucepan until melted. Stir in 1 teaspoon of the vanilla extract. Spoon into a heatproof bowl. Chill for 2 hours, stirring occasionally.

Cut the bananas into ¼-inch slices, arranging over the chocolate layer. Spread the vanilla custard over the bananas. Chill for 2 to 12 hours or until set.

Whip the remaining 1 cup cream, powdered sugar and remaining 1 teaspoon vanilla extract in a mixing bowl until soft peaks form. Spread over the pie. Chill for 20 minutes or until serving time. Shave the remaining 1 ounce of chocolate over the pie using a vegetable peeler. Sprinkle with the almonds.

Mason Jar Key Lime Pies

SERVES 8

8 half-pint Mason jars
½ cup graham cracker crumbs
2 tablespoons butter, melted
2 tablespoons sugar
5 egg yolks, beaten
½ cup Key lime juice
   (about 12 to 15 limes)

1 (14-ounce) can sweetened
   condensed milk
Coconut Whipped Cream
   (recipe below)
2 teaspoons grated Key lime zest
   (optional)

Preheat the oven to 350 degrees. Spray the inside of the Mason jars with nonstick cooking spray. Arrange the jars in a small baking pan.

Combine the graham cracker crumbs, butter and sugar in a bowl and mix well. Press 1 heaping tablespoonful of the mixture over the bottom of each prepared jar, reserving any remaining mixture. Bake for 3 minutes. Let stand to cool.

Whisk the egg yolks, Key lime juice and sweetened condensed milk in a bowl until blended. Divide evenly among the jars. Bake for 8 to 10 minutes or just until set but not firm. Let stand to cool completely. Dollop or pipe equal portions of the Coconut Whipped Cream into each jar. Sprinkle with the reserved graham cracker mixture and Key lime zest. Chill until serving time.

COCONUT WHIPPED CREAM

1 cup heavy whipping cream
½ cup canned coconut milk
   (white part only)
2 tablespoons powdered sugar

Beat the whipping cream, coconut milk and powdered sugar at medium-high speed in a mixing bowl until soft peaks form.

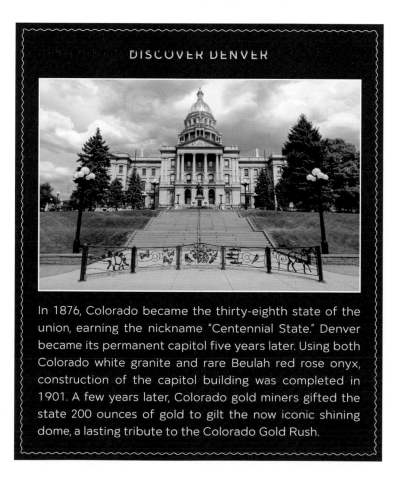

DISCOVER DENVER

In 1876, Colorado became the thirty-eighth state of the union, earning the nickname "Centennial State." Denver became its permanent capitol five years later. Using both Colorado white granite and rare Beulah red rose onyx, construction of the capitol building was completed in 1901. A few years later, Colorado gold miners gifted the state 200 ounces of gold to gilt the now iconic shining dome, a lasting tribute to the Colorado Gold Rush.

Plum Strawberry Pie

SERVES 8

1 package refrigerated piecrust
4 cups plum slices (¼ to ½ inch)
2 cups strawberries slices
  (¼ to ½ inch)
Juice of ½ medium lemon
¾ cup plus 1 tablespoon sugar,
  divided

½ cup all-purpose flour
¼ teaspoon salt
¼ teaspoon ground cinnamon
⅛ teaspoon ground nutmeg
1 tablespoon half-and-half

Preheat the oven to 375 degrees. Roll each piecrust into an 11-inch circle. Fit 1 of the piecrusts into a 9-inch pie plate, trimming the edge.

Combine the plums, strawberries and lemon juice in a large bowl and toss to coat. Combine ¾ cup of the sugar, flour, salt, cinnamon and nutmeg in a medium bowl. Pour over the plum mixture and stir to coat. Spoon into the prepared pie plate. Cut the remaining piecrust into long thin strips or cut using cookie cutters. Place the strips on the pie in a lattice pattern or overlap the shapes over the pie, leaving a few vents. Brush with the half-and half. Sprinkle with the remaining 1 tablespoon sugar. Bake for 10 minutes. Cover the edge with a crust shield or foil ring. Bake for 30 minutes longer or until golden brown and bubbly. Let stand to cool completely. Serve à la mode if desired.

Entertaining Tip

Set and decorate your table the night or morning before a large gathering. This lets you focus on the food and your guests the day of the event.

Pumpkin Pie with Gingersnap Crust and Sugared Cranberries

SERVES 8

8 ounces gingersnaps
¼ cup unsalted butter, melted
1 cup pumpkin purée
2 cups whipping cream, divided
1 cup packed brown sugar
2 eggs

½ teaspoon salt
½ teaspoon ground cinnamon
½ teaspoon freshly grated or ground nutmeg
¼ teaspoon ground cloves
¼ teaspoon ground ginger

¼ teaspoon allspice
2 tablespoons bourbon
2 tablespoons granulated sugar
¼ cup pecans, finely chopped (optional)
Sugared Cranberries (recipe below)

Process the gingersnaps in a food processor until fine crumbs form. Melt the butter in a small saucepan. Bring to a gentle boil. Cook until the butter is golden brown and smells nutty, swirling the saucepan slowly. Pour over the gingersnaps in the food processor and pulse until blended. Press over the bottom and side of a 9-inch pie plate. Chill for 15 minutes.

Preheat the oven to 325 degrees.

Bake the pie shell for 15 minutes. Increase the oven temperature to 350 degrees.

Combine the pumpkin, 1 cup of the cream, brown sugar, eggs, salt, cinnamon, nutmeg, cloves, ginger and allspice in a large bowl and mix well. Spoon into the piecrust. Bake for 45 minutes or until the center is set, covering the crust with foil if browning too quickly. Cool on a wire rack.

Beat the remaining 1 cup cream in a mixing bowl using the whip attachment until soft peaks form, starting on low speed and increasing the speed gradually. Add the bourbon and granulated sugar. Beat at medium speed until stiff peaks form. Sprinkle the pie with the pecans and Sugared Cranberries. Garnish with decorative shapes of baked pie pastry. Serve with the whipped cream.

SUGARED CRANBERRIES

2 cups sugar, divided
½ cup water

12 ounces fresh cranberries

Combine ½ cup of the sugar and water in a small saucepan. Cook over medium heat until the sugar is dissolved, stirring frequently. Remove from the heat. Add the cranberries and stir to coat completely. Spread in a single layer on a wire rack or parchment paper. Let stand for 1 hour or until dry but sticky. Place the remaining 1½ cups sugar in a large bowl. Add the cranberries in batches and toss gently to coat, arranging on a clean wire rack or parchment paper. Let stand for 1 hour or longer.

Almond, Apricot and Cream Cheese Crostata

SERVES 8

1 (9-inch) refrigerated piecrust,
   at room temperature
3½ ounces almond paste
4 tablespoons sugar, divided
1 egg, separated
3 ounces cream cheese, softened

1 teaspoon pure vanilla extract
¼ cup apricot jam
6 medium fresh apricots, cut into
   fourths
1 teaspoon water

Preheat the oven to 400 degrees. Line a baking sheet with parchment paper. Unroll the piecrust on the parchment paper.

Process the almond paste, 3 tablespoons of the sugar, egg yolk, cream cheese and vanilla extract in a food processor until smooth. Spread over the piecrust, leaving a 1½-inch border. Heat the apricot jam in a small saucepan over low heat. Arrange the apricots peeling sides down over the filling. Brush with the apricot jam. Fold the piecrust border over the filling to form a crust.

Beat the egg white and water in a small bowl. Brush over the piecrust border. Sprinkle the filling and crust with the remaining 1 tablespoon sugar. Bake for 40 to 45 minutes or until the crust is brown and the apricots are tender, covering the crust with a foil ring if needed to prevent overbrowning. Let stand to cool slightly before serving.

DISCOVER DENVER

Denver's commitment to public art is evident along Cherry Creek Trail, one of the city's most popular pedestrian and bike paths. The forty-mile trail begins downtown at Confluence Park and travels through historic neighborhoods, old stagecoach stops, and Castlewood Canyon State Park.

Apple Cranberry Crisp with Maple Whipped Cream

SERVES 8

4 medium apples (such as Fuji)
2 tablespoons sugar
1 teaspoon ground cinnamon
1 (14-ounce) can whole
　cranberry sauce
1 cup packed light brown sugar

1 cup old-fashioned oats
¾ cup all-purpose flour
⅛ teaspoon salt
½ cup cold butter, thinly sliced
Maple Whipped Cream (recipe below)

Preheat the oven to 350 degrees. Spray a cast-iron skillet or 8×8-inch baking dish with nonstick cooking spray.

Peel the apples and cut into ½-inch pieces. Place the apples in the prepared baking dish. Toss with the sugar and cinnamon. Add the cranberry sauce and stir to mix.

Combine the brown sugar, oats, flour and salt in a bowl and mix well. Sprinkle over the apple mixture. Arrange the butter slices in a single layer over the top. Bake for 1 hour or until brown and bubbly and the apples are tender. Serve warm with the Maple Whipped Cream.

MAPLE WHIPPED CREAM

2 cups heavy whipping cream
2 tablespoons powdered sugar

1 teaspoon maple extract

Beat the whipping cream in a large mixing bowl until soft peaks form, starting at low speed and increasing the speed gradually. Add the powdered sugar and maple extract. Beat at medium speed until stiff peaks form.

Brandy Prune and Apple Crumble

SERVES 8

1 cup pitted prunes
¾ cup brandy
⅔ cup all-purpose flour
6 tablespoons packed
    light brown sugar
6 tablespoons cold unsalted butter,
    cut into small pieces

¼ teaspoon kosher salt
¼ teaspoon ground cinnamon
⅔ cup old-fashioned oats
6 medium baking apples, peeled and
    cut into quarters
2 tablespoons granulated sugar

Preheat the oven to 425 degrees. Butter a 1½-quart baking dish.

Combine the prunes and brandy in a saucepan. Bring to a boil over medium heat; do not cover. Turn off the heat, keeping the saucepan in place. Pulse the flour, brown sugar, butter, salt and cinnamon in a food processor until the mixture resembles coarse meal. Add the oats and pulse just until mixed.

Spread the apples in the prepared baking dish. Sprinkle with the granulated sugar. Spoon the prune mixture over the apples. Sprinkle with the flour mixture. Bake, covered with foil, for 25 minutes. Bake, uncovered, until golden brown. Serve warm with ice cream, whipped cream or warm custard.

DISCOVER DENVER

The Denver Art Museum is one of the largest art museums in the Western US. It is recognized not only for the vast collection of over 70,000 works of art contained within its walls but also for the unique architecture that defines its exterior. The North Building, which resembles a fort protecting the art within, is the only completed project in the US by famed Italian designer Gio Ponti. The sharp edges and angles of the Frederic C. Hamilton Building, designed by architect Daniel Libeskind, were inspired by the peaks and geological formations of the Rocky Mountains.

Rhubarb Blueberry Cobbler with Pistachio Topping

Favorite recipe from Colorado Colore chosen by Editors Alissa Gutin West and Wendy Zerr

SERVES 6 TO 8

½ cup sugar
3 tablespoons all-purpose flour
2 cups fresh or frozen chopped
   rhubarb

2 cups fresh blueberries
2 tablespoons lemon juice
Pistachio Topping (recipe below)

Preheat the oven to 375 degrees. Spray a 2-quart baking dish with nonstick cooking spray.

Combine the sugar and flour in a large bowl and mix well. Add the rhubarb and blueberries and mix gently. Stir in the lemon juice. Spoon into the prepared baking dish. Squeeze the Pistachio Topping together a handful at a time and crumble coarsely over the rhubarb mixture. Bake for 40 minutes or until brown and bubbly.

PISTACHIO TOPPING

¾ cup all-purpose flour
⅓ cup granulated sugar
⅓ cup packed brown sugar

6 tablespoons cold unsalted butter,
   cut into cubes
⅓ cup pistachios, finely chopped

Combine the flour, granulated sugar and brown sugar in a bowl and mix well. Cut in the butter with a pastry blender until crumbly. Stir in the pistachios.

Published in 2002, *Colorado Colore* is a selection of recipes designed to be artfully inspiring, yet uncomplicated and accessible.

"Food is a fun adventure and brings people together, whether with family or when entertaining friends.Sure, we ate, slept, and breathed this project, but bringing our various experiences, backgrounds, and talents to the table allowed us to pull it all together, and we hope it has brought our readers and their families and friends together as well."
—Alissa Gutin West and Wendy Zerr

Pumpkin Cheesecake

SERVES 8

1½ cups graham cracker crumbs
1½ cups granulated sugar, divided
⅓ cup butter, melted
24 ounces cream cheese, softened
¼ cup packed light brown sugar

1 (16-ounce) can pumpkin purée
2 eggs
⅔ cup evaporated milk
2 tablespoons cornstarch
1¼ teaspoons ground cinnamon

½ teaspoon ground nutmeg
2 cups sour cream, at room
 temperature
1 teaspoon vanilla extract

Preheat the oven to 350 degrees.

Combine the graham cracker crumbs, ¼ cup of the granulated sugar and butter in a medium bowl and mix well. Press over the bottom and 1 inch up the side of a 9-inch springform pan. Bake for 6 to 8 minutes; do not burn. Let stand to cool.

Beat the cream cheese, 1 cup of the granulated sugar and brown sugar in a large mixing bowl until fluffy. Beat in the pumpkin, eggs and evaporated milk. Add the cornstarch, cinnamon and nutmeg and mix well. Spoon into the prepared crust. Bake for 55 to 60 minutes or until the edge is set.

Combine the sour cream, remaining ¼ cup granulated sugar and vanilla extract in a small bowl and mix well. Spread over the cheesecake. Bake for 5 minutes. Let stand to cool on a wire rack. Remove the side of the pan. Chill for 6 to 12 hours.

Mile High Cheesecake

SERVES 8

¾ cup graham cracker crumbs
4 tablespoons butter, melted
32 ounces cream cheese, softened
5 eggs
1½ cups sugar, divided

½ cup all-purpose flour
1 tablespoon fresh lemon juice
5 teaspoons vanilla extract, divided
2 cups sour cream
1 (12-ounce) jar raspberry jelly

1 tablespoon cornstarch
1 quart large strawberries,
 stems removed

Preheat the oven to 350 degrees.

Combine the graham cracker crumbs and butter in a bowl and mix well. Press over the bottom of a 10-inch springform pan. Beat the cream cheese, eggs, 1¼ cups of the sugar, flour, lemon juice and 4 teaspoons of the vanilla extract in a mixing bowl until blended. Spread over the crust. Place the pan on a baking sheet. Bake for 50 to 55 minutes. Let stand to cool slightly.

Combine the sour cream, remaining ¼ cup sugar and remaining 1 teaspoon vanilla extract in a bowl and mix well. Spread over the cheesecake, leaving a ½-inch border. Bake for 5 minutes. Chill for 12 to 24 hours.

Combine the raspberry jelly and cornstarch in a saucepan. Cook over medium heat for 5 minutes or until the glaze is translucent, stirring occasionally. Arrange the strawberries stemmed sides down around the outer edge of the cheesecake. Drizzle the glaze over the cheesecake and strawberries just before serving.

Chocolate Pavlova

SERVES 8

6 egg whites, at room temperature
1¾ cups plus 2 tablespoons sugar,
 divided
3 tablespoons baking cocoa

1 teaspoon balsamic vinegar
⅛ teaspoon sea salt
2 ounces dark chocolate,
 finely chopped

1¾ cups heavy whipping cream
3 cups raspberries or other berries
2 ounces semisweet chocolate

Preheat the oven to 350 degrees. Line a baking sheet with parchment paper. Trace a 9-inch cake pan on the paper using a pencil or pen. Turn the paper over.

Whip the egg whites at high speed in a mixing bowl with the whisk attachment until soft peaks form. Add 1¾ cups of the sugar gradually, beating constantly. Beat until the meringue is stiff and shiny. Sprinkle the baking cocoa, vinegar and sea salt over the egg white. Add the dark chocolate and fold in with a rubber spatula until well mixed; some streaks may remain. Mound the meringue onto the paper circle, smoothing the top and side with the spatula. Place in the oven. Reduce the oven temperature to 300 degrees. Bake the meringue for 1 hour or until dry and crisp; center may be slightly soft. Turn off the oven and open the door slightly. Let the meringue cool completely in the oven. May be made up to this point 1 day ahead. Store, loosely covered, at room temperature.

Whip the cream in a mixing bowl using the whisk attachment until soft peaks form. Add the remaining 2 tablespoons sugar and whip until incorporated. Remove and discard the parchment paper from the meringue. Place the meringue on a large plate. Spread the whipped cream over the meringue, leaving a 1½-inch border. Scatter the raspberries over the whipped cream. Shave the semisweet chocolate over the top. Serve immediately.

Entertaining Tip

An edible ink pen can turn almost any cookie into an adorable place card for your next event. Just choose any store-bought or homemade cookies with smooth crusty tops, and write your guests' names in edible ink!

BLACKBERRY SORBET

Blackberry Sorbet

SERVES 4

2½ cups fresh blackberries
½ cup water
1¼ cups sugar

Juice of 1 lemon
1 tablespoon vodka

Process the blackberries and water in a blender until smooth. Strain through a fine mesh sieve into a stainless-steel bowl, discarding the seeds. Add the sugar, lemon juice and vodka. Place the bowl in a larger bowl of ice water. Stir until the sugar is dissolved. Leave in the ice bath until the mixture reaches 40 degrees on a candy thermometer. Freeze in an ice cream maker following the manufacturer's directions. Remove to a freezer-safe container. Freeze for several hours or up to 1 week. May skip the use of the ice cream maker; results will not be as creamy. Garnish servings with mint leaves.

Monster Cookies

MAKES 6 DOZEN

1½ cups peanut butter
1⅓ cups packed brown sugar
1 cup granulated sugar
½ cup butter
3 eggs
2 teaspoons baking soda

1½ teaspoons light corn syrup
1½ teaspoons vanilla extract
4½ cups old-fashioned oats
12 ounces miniature chocolate chips
1 (11-ounce) package candy-coated
  chocolates

Preheat the oven to 350 degrees.

Combine the peanut butter, brown sugar, granulated sugar and butter in a mixing bowl. Beat until blended. Add the eggs, baking soda, corn syrup and vanilla extract and mix well. Stir in the oats. Add the chocolate chips and mix well. Drop by tablespoonfuls onto baking sheets. Sprinkle with the candy-coated chocolates. Bake for 12 to 15 minutes or until golden brown. Let stand to cool for 2 minutes. Remove the cookies to wire racks. Let stand to cool completely.

Irish Stout Chocolate Chunk Cookies

MAKES 3 DOZEN

2 (11-ounce) bottles Guinness® or
    other dry Irish stout
1 cup packed brown sugar, divided
2 ¾ cups all-purpose flour
½ cup baking cocoa
1 ½ teaspoons instant espresso
    powder
¾ teaspoon baking soda

½ teaspoon salt
1 cup granulated sugar
½ cup unsalted butter
½ cup shortening
2 eggs
1 teaspoon vanilla extract
1 ½ cups white chocolate chunks
1 ½ cups semisweet chocolate chunks

Simmer the stout and ½ cup of the brown sugar in a saucepan over medium heat for 40 to 45 minutes or until thickened and reduced to about ⅔ cup. Let stand to cool slightly.

Preheat the oven to 350 degrees. Line 2 baking sheets with parchment paper.

Whisk the flour, baking cocoa, espresso powder, baking soda and salt in a bowl. Beat the granulated sugar, butter, shortening and remaining ½ cup brown sugar at medium speed in a large mixing bowl for 3 minutes or until fluffy. Add the stout mixture, eggs and vanilla extract and mix well. Stir in the flour mixture just until incorporated. Fold in the white chocolate and semisweet chocolate.

Shape 2 tablespoonfuls of the dough at a time into balls, arranging on the prepared baking sheets. Bake for 12 to 14 minutes or until the edges are set. Let stand to cool for 2 minutes. Remove the cookies to wire racks. Let stand to cool completely.

Gingerbread Cookie Edible Ornaments

MAKES 6 TO 7 DOZEN

3 cups all-purpose flour, sifted
½ cup natural unsweetened baking cocoa, sifted
½ teaspoon baking soda
¼ teaspoon baking powder
2 teaspoons ground ginger
2 teaspoons ground cinnamon

1 teaspoon ground cloves
½ teaspoon ground mace
½ teaspoon salt
¼ teaspoon ground black pepper
½ cup packed dark brown sugar
½ cup unsalted butter, softened
2 eggs, lightly whisked

¼ cup unsulphured molasses
1 bottle decorative sugar crystals (optional)
Edible sugar pearls to taste (optional)
Edible gold dust (optional)

Sift the flour, baking cocoa, baking soda, baking powder, ginger, cinnamon, cloves, mace, salt and pepper into a large mixing bowl. Beat the brown sugar and butter in a large mixing bowl with the paddle attachment for 2 minutes or until light and smooth. Add the eggs in a steady stream, beating constantly. Beat until light and fluffy. Add the molasses and mix well, scraping the side of the bowl occasionally. Add the flour mixture and mix until incorporated. Cut the dough into halves and shape into balls. Place each ball on a piece of plastic wrap and flatten slightly. Wrap with the plastic wrap. Chill for 1 hour or longer.

Preheat the oven to 350 degrees, moving the oven rack to the top position.

Roll each portion of the dough ¼ inch thick on a lightly floured surface using a floured rolling pin; dough will be sticky at first. Cut using a 3-inch cookie cutter, arranging evenly spaced on a baking sheet using a spatula. Sprinkle with the sugar crystals, pressing lightly into the dough.

May make a hole at the top of each cookie using the flat round end of a wooden cake tester and fill the hole with an edible sugar pearl or leave the hole for adding a ribbon later for a table name card or an edible tree ornament. Chill for 15 minutes.

Bake for 7 to 8 minutes for ornaments, allowing less baking time for softer cookies. Brush with edible gold dust. Remove to wire racks to cool.

Hazelnut Brown Butter Chocolate Chip Cookies

MAKES 2 DOZEN

2 ¼ cups all-purpose flour
1 ¼ teaspoons baking soda
¼ teaspoon salt
1 cup unsalted butter
1 cup packed dark brown sugar

¼ cup granulated sugar
1 egg plus 1 egg yolk
2 teaspoons vanilla extract
1 tablespoon plain Greek yogurt
½ cup semisweet chocolate chips

½ cup milk chocolate chips
¼ cup dark chocolate chips
1 cup cold hazelnut chocolate spread
Coarse sea salt

Whisk the flour, baking soda and ¼ teaspoon salt in a bowl. Cook the butter in a saucepan over medium heat just until foamy, whisking constantly. Cook until brown and smells nutty, whisking constantly. Pour into a bowl. Let stand to cool.

Combine the brown sugar and granulated sugar in a mixing bowl. Add the butter carefully, discarding the brown bits at the bottom of the bowl. Beat until well mixed. Add the egg, egg yolk, vanilla extract and yogurt and beat until mixed. Add the flour mixture gradually, beating constantly at low speed just until incorporated. Fold in the semisweet chocolate chips, milk chocolate chips and dark chocolate chips. Chill the dough for 2 hours, or freeze for 30 minutes.

Preheat the oven to 350 degrees.

Shape the dough by 2 tablespoonfuls into balls and flatten between palms. Spoon 1 teaspoonful of hazelnut chocolate spread onto each, folding the dough into a ball to fully enclose and arranging 2 inches apart on a baking sheet; flatten gently. Bake for 9 to 11 minutes or just until the edges are golden brown; cookies will appear underdone but will continue to cook. Let stand to cool for a few minutes. Sprinkle each with a small amount of sea salt. Remove to wire racks to cool.

Entertaining Tip

Invite guests into a different space for a sweet bite or a cup of coffee after the meal. Changing locations keeps guests from getting tired, allows connections with other guests, and encourages them to linger longer.

A Peach of a Cookie

MAKES 2 DOZEN

3 ½ cups all-purpose flour
1 tablespoon baking powder
3 eggs
¾ cup sugar
½ cup milk
½ cup unsalted butter, melted
    and cooled

Grated zest of 1 large orange
1 cup mascarpone cheese
¼ cup peach preserves
½ cup clear liquor (such as peach
    schnapps, rum or vodka), divided
4 drops (about) red food coloring,
    divided

3 drops (about) yellow food coloring
2 cups ultrafine baker's sugar
Small leaves of 1 bunch mint

Preheat the oven to 350 degrees. Line 2 baking sheets with silicone mats or parchment paper.

Sift the flour and baking powder into a large bowl. Whisk the eggs and sugar in a bowl until pale yellow. Whisk in the milk, butter and orange zest until smooth. Add the flour mixture a third at a time, stirring gently with a rubber spatula to incorporate after each addition. Mix with hands until a sticky dough forms. Cover with plastic wrap. Let stand for 5 minutes.

Shape the dough into 48 cherry-size balls using floured hands, arranging 1 inch apart on the prepared baking sheets. Bake 1 baking sheet at a time for 12 to 14 minutes or just until the bottoms of the cookies are golden brown. Remove to a wire rack. Let stand to cool. Scoop out a ¼-inch-deep circle in the bottom of each cookie using a small pointed spoon, working carefully and reserving the cookie crumbs.

Crumble the reserved cookie crumbs into small consistent crumbs into a medium bowl. Add the mascarpone cheese and peach preserves and mix into a paste. Spoon or pipe a small amount of the filling into each hollow cookie, filling to just above the bottom of the cookie. Match each cookie to a cookie of similar size, creating a sandwich and wiping off any excess filling.

Pour ¼ cup of the liquor into each of 2 bowls. Add 3 drops of red food coloring to 1 of the bowls. Add 3 drops of yellow food coloring and 1 drop of red food coloring to the remaining bowl and stir to make the color orange. Place the baker's sugar in a deep bowl. Brush half of each cookie with orange coloring and the other half with red coloring; the colors will merge. Place each "peach" immediately into the baker's sugar and shake the bowl to cover the cookie, being careful not to touch the cookies with wet fingers or the sugar will clump. Remove the cookies to a large tray. Let stand until dry. May be made up to 4 days ahead and stored in the refrigerator. Allow to come to room temperature. Add a mint sprig to each cookie to resemble peach leaves just before serving.

Lemon Ricotta Cookies

MAKES ABOUT 3 DOZEN

4 cups all-purpose flour
1 teaspoon baking powder
½ teaspoon baking soda
½ teaspoon salt
1 cup unsalted butter, softened

2 cups granulated sugar
15 ounces ricotta cheese, at room
    temperature
Grated zest of 1 medium lemon
2 eggs

3 teaspoons vanilla extract,
    divided
2 cups powdered sugar
Juice of ½ medium lemon

Preheat the oven to 350 degrees. Line a baking sheet with parchment paper.

Combine the flour, baking powder, baking soda and salt in a bowl and mix well. Cream the butter and granulated sugar in a large mixing bowl. Add the ricotta cheese and lemon zest and mix well. Add the eggs gradually, beating constantly. Beat in 2 teaspoons of the vanilla extract. Add the flour mixture gradually, beating well after each addition. Shape by 1 or 1½ tablespoonfuls into balls using floured hands, arranging 2 inches apart on the prepared baking sheets and pressing into disks. Bake in batches for 10 to 12 minutes or just until golden brown and the centers are set. Let stand to cool for 2 minutes. Remove to wire racks to cool completely, placing waxed paper under the racks.

Combine the powdered sugar, lemon juice and remaining 1 teaspoon vanilla extract in a bowl and stir until shiny white and slightly thickened. Spread or drizzle over each cookie.

Almond Bars

MAKES 2 DOZEN

7 ounces almond paste
1 cup unsalted butter, softened
2 cups granulated sugar
½ teaspoon almond extract
½ teaspoon salt

2 eggs
2 cups all-purpose flour
½ cup sliced almonds
1 tablespoon coarse or
    raw sugar (optional)

Preheat the oven to 350 degrees. Grease a 9×13-inch glass baking dish.

Break the almond paste into smaller pieces in a large mixing bowl. Add the butter and beat until creamy. Add the granulated sugar gradually, beating constantly. Beat until light and fluffy. Add the almond extract and salt and mix well. Add the eggs one at a time alternately with the flour 1 cup at a time, beating constantly. Spread in the prepared baking dish. Sprinkle with the almonds, pressing lightly into the dough. Sprinkle with the coarse sugar. Bake for 25 to 30 minutes or until golden brown and the center is set. Let stand to cool completely before cutting into bars.

Almond Raspberry Bars

Favorite recipe from Colorado Classique chosen by Cookbook Chair Stephanie Duncan

MAKES 35

2 ½ cups all-purpose flour, divided
½ cup powdered sugar
1 ¼ cups cold unsalted butter, divided

2 cups raspberry preserves
¼ cup Chambord liqueur
¼ cup granulated sugar

7 ounces almond paste
⅔ cup sliced almonds
Vanilla Icing (recipe below)

Preheat the oven to 350 degrees. Grease a 9×13-inch glass baking dish.

Combine 2 cups of the flour, powdered sugar and 1 cup of the butter in a food processor and pulse until crumbly. Press over the bottom of the prepared baking dish. Bake for 20 minutes or until light golden brown. Maintain oven temperature.

Combine the raspberry preserves and liqueur in a bowl and mix well. Spread over the crust. Combine the remaining ½ cup flour, granulated sugar, almond paste and remaining ¼ cup butter in the food processor and pulse until crumbly. Sprinkle over the raspberry mixture. Sprinkle with the almonds. Bake for 40 minutes or until golden brown. Let stand to cool on a wire rack; filling will set as it cools. Drizzle with the Vanilla Icing. Chill until completely cooled before cutting into bars with a sharp knife.

VANILLA ICING

1 cup powdered sugar
3 tablespoons milk

1 teaspoon vanilla extract

Combine the powdered sugar, milk and vanilla extract in a bowl and mix well.

Published in 2009, *Colorado Classique* features a collection of over 200 fresh recipes from the casual Après Ski Beans to the elegant Truffled Gnocchi, beer and wine pairings, beautiful photography, and a Colorado restaurant chapter.

Salted Caramel Bars

MAKES 28

1 (14-ounce) can sweetened
   condensed milk
2 cups butter, softened
1 cup granulated sugar

1½ cups powdered sugar
1 tablespoon vanilla extract
3½ cups all-purpose flour
2 teaspoons coarsely ground sea salt

Pour the sweetened condensed milk into a pint-size canning jar and cover with the lid. Place in a slow cooker. Add enough water to reach just below the bottom of the lid. Cook on Low for 8 hours. Remove the jar carefully from the slow cooker. Let stand to cool completely; caramel will thicken as it cools.

Preheat the oven to 350 degrees. Spray a 9×13-inch glass baking dish with nonstick cooking spray.

Cream the butter, granulated sugar and powdered sugar in a mixing bowl. Add the vanilla extract and mix well. Add the flour ½ cup at a time, beating until incorporated after each addition. Cut the dough into halves. Wrap 1 half in plastic wrap and place in the refrigerator. Press the remaining dough over the bottom of the prepared baking dish. Bake for 20 minutes or until the edges are light golden brown. Let stand to cool for 15 minutes. Maintain oven temperature.

Pour the caramel over the crust. Sprinkle with the sea salt. Crumble the chilled dough into pea- to marble-size pieces over the caramel. Bake for 25 to 30 minutes or until golden brown. Sprinkle with additional sea salt if desired.

Vanilla Bean Marshmallows

MAKES 32

¼ cup (about) powdered sugar, divided
2 vanilla beans
1 tablespoon vanilla extract
½ cup ice water

3 envelopes unflavored gelatin
1½ cups granulated sugar
1 cup light corn syrup
½ cup water, at room temperature
¼ teaspoon salt

Spray an 8×8-inch dish lightly with nonstick spray. Dust with a small amount of the powdered sugar using a sieve. Split the vanilla beans lengthwise into halves. Remove the seeds using the flat side of a small paring knife. Combine the seeds and vanilla extract in a small bowl.

Pour the ice water over the gelatin in a mixing bowl fitted with the whisk attachment. Let stand to dissolve. Combine the granulated sugar, corn syrup, room temperature water and salt in a heavy saucepan. Cook over medium heat until the sugar is dissolved, stirring constantly. Increase the heat to high. Cook until the mixture reaches 240 degrees on a candy thermometer at sea level or 230 degrees at 5,000 feet above sea level, soft-ball stage; be sure the thermometer is fully submerged. Remove from the heat.

Beat the dissolved gelatin at low speed, adding the hot sugar mixture gradually. Increase the speed to high. Whip the mixture for 8 minutes or until very thick and slightly cooled. Add the vanilla mixture and beat at low speed until well mixed. Pour into the prepared dish. Dust with a small amount of the powdered sugar. Let stand, uncovered, for 4 hours. Remove to a cutting board dusted with powdered sugar. Cut the marshmallows into 32 squares or rectangles using a pizza cutter or sharp knife dusted with powdered sugar. Dust the marshmallows with powdered sugar. Let stand, uncovered, for 4 to 12 hours. Store in an airtight container.

Thank you to our Corporate Sponsors!

SILVER SPOON

FRIENDS OF THE JUNIOR LEAGUE

DES MOINES

Falvey Properties

Thank you to our Major In-Kind Donors!

Amanda Wright Pottery
Patricia Bainter
Christine Dupont-Patz
Tracy and Darren Gibbons
Paulette and Jim Guion

Katie, Adam, and
   Matilda Harmon
Karl Heintz at The Antique
   Exchange Co-Op
Cathy Hollis

Ashley and Kamil Keski
Wendy and Steve Lowe
Mary Beth and Michael McErlane
Stacey Rubinstein
Becky and Brian Schaub

Thank you to our Underwriting Donors!

$2,500

Margie & George Browning
Lauren O'Neill Crist-Fulk

Barbara H. Ferguson
Jill Pedicord Peterson

Laura Stenovec

$1,000

Sherri Koelbel in memory of
   Gene Norgren Koelbel
Barbara W. Pierce

Jennifer Pomeroy-Fronk
Becky & Brian Schaub
Cille B. Williams

Nancy S. Wright in memory of
   Margaret Seacrest

$500

Stephany Bollin in memory of
   Kristina Kelso
Kristin & Stephen Brownson in
   memory of Ginny Hartman
Trish Delano

Ginny Fuller & JLD Gourmet
   Group in honor of Jaydee Boat
Arlene & Barry Hirschfeld
Cathy & Graham Hollis
Janie Hutchison
Jan Ann Kahler

Malia and Derek Keck
Deanna H. Person
Catherine Hoover Petros
Becky Schaub in honor of the
   Colorado Classique Steering
   Committee

$250

Karen Albin
Michele Austin
Joe & Shannon Batal
Joann Morgan Burstein
Kelsey Cochrane
Kendall "Kendy" Cusick-Rindone
Carleigh Landers Elkus
Christine Fedorowicz
Debbie Frei
Cornelia M. Gibson
Abby Gilbertson

Jessica Grimes
Karen Gutierrez
Anne K. Hackstock
Ms. Beverlee Henry
Kaye Isaacs
Patty L. Mack
Carole McCotter
Adrienne & Tom McNamara
Diane Newcom
Laurene B. Owen
Team Rissmiller
Melanie Milam Roth

Jennifer Rothschild
Kathleen B. Sorensen
Christine Guin Spencer
Stan & Sandi Sprinkle
Summit Wealth Advisors
Nancy Tankersley
Wendy Trigg
Alissa Twiss
Marjory A. Ulm
Flossie Walter
Lee Wyma & Courteney Keatinge

$100

Lora M. Adams
Carole Adelstein in honor of the
   2017-18 Garden Club Board
Laurie Althen
Margaret Ansted in honor of
   Andrea Hoffman

Katy Daniel Arnold in memory
   of Sally Daniel
Marjorie Callahan
Karen T. Cohn
Kayla D. Dreyer, Esq.
Nancy Bauer Egelhoff in memory
   of Jean Kunze Sullivan

Mr. & Mrs. Christopher Elliott
Anne & Jeff Fajkus
Melinda Fisher
Mary-Katherine Brooks Fleming in
   honor of Violet Estrella Fleming,
   born 1/26/18

Janie H. Fletcher
Barb Goettelman
Judy Wong Greco
Alana Hancock in honor of
David & Alana Hancock
Nora Heitmann
Susie Houston
Bev Howell in memory of
Donna Hultin
Liz Johnson
Ali J. Kaiser
Julia Kneeland Lazure
Ashley Legler in honor of
Parks Louise Legler

Mamie Ling
Susan Warner McCann in
memory of Barbara Miller
Caryne E. Mesquita
Susan H. Moore
Susan Ayers Phelps
Marti B. Potter
Natalie Newcom Ralston in
honor of Diane Newcom
Lindsey Russell
Alyssa Russo in honor of
Rachel Jauregui
Sally Russo
Cheryl Smith
Ronda Barlow Smith

Colette G. Sutley in honor of
Hannon Elizabeth Sutley
Sonnie Talley
Julie Taylor
Lee Tedstrom in memory of
Mary Poole
Lee Tedstrom in memory of
Jancy Campbell
Ann Tull
Jacklyn VanOoyik
Kimberly Vestal
Laurel Walk
Barbara J. Webb
Pamela Weber
Megan Whelan

$50

Angela & Scarlett Andrews
Vanessa M. Banker in honor of
Matthew & Kiedis Ingram
Jerilyn J. Bensard
Grace Devlin Bird in memory of
Joann Devlin Roath
Teresa Tahir Blount
Jaydee Boat
Lynn Buhrmeister
Mara Buhrmeister
Sandy Clanahan in memory of
Chartan Martin
Lauren O'Neill Crist-Fulk in
honor of O'Neill Watts
Elizabeth L. Crites
Joanne Davidson
Melanie Lewis Dickerson
Tina Downs
Fay Pearson Dreher
The Enright Family in memory
of Terry Enright
J. Inge Fox-Jones

J. Inge Fox-Jones in memory
of Else M. Fox
Sharon A. Hartman in memory
of Patricia P. Hartman
Andrew & Bonnie Hill in honor
of Millie Kay Hill
Preston Hodges Hill in memory
of Peggy Harrison
Amy Jaynes
Christy Jordan in honor of
Nancy Winters Jordan &
Sally Winters Rippey
Christy Jordan in honor of my
future JLD daughters
Molly & Kate Jordan Little
Maureen Keefner
Ashley Moery Keski in honor of
the fearless Moery women
Ana (Sandomire) Koser
Stephanie (Taffy) Leonard
Mary Lester in memory of
Joyce Metz
Katie Mata

Karen Mayo in honor of my foodie
family Ron, Zachary & Emily
Mary Beth & Michael McErlane in
honor of Sophie McErlane
Mariette E. Moore in honor of
Deborah A. Moore
Helen Ruth Mozer
Karen Parry
Pam Piro
Jill Boat Rakowski
Ann Roemer
Carole Rollins
Aline Sandomire
Megan Severs
Casse Silva
Marjie Skalet in honor of
Mimi Nelson
Lindsey Talafuse in honor of
Tenley Talafuse
Sonnie Talley
Kristen and Jim Warnick
Lauren Whitney

Thank you to our Recipe Submitters!

Corinne Ablin
Adair Ahlers
Robin Andersen
Robin Arnett
Katy Daniel Arnold
Heather Ashour
Patricia Bainter
Mari Banka
Patricia Barrie
Gracie Batt
Sarah Battey
Erin Beimford
Leslie Berry
Maureen Berry
Aimee Bianca
Diane Bierbach
Grace Bird
Dave Bishop
Kelsey Blair
Stephen Blaisdell
Teresa Blount
Wendy Boedeker
Kirsten Boyd
Jean and Walt Boylan
Leah Bradley
Kathy Brooks
Barbara Brown
Patricia Brown
Caroline Brownson
Kristin Brownson
Stephen Brownson
Linda Brune
Nonie Brzyski
Adele Burnham
Cissie Megyesy Busch
Samantha Butterworth
Sean Cameron
Jennifer Caparrelli
Christy Chalk
Diane Cheatwood
Elizabeth Dilorenzo Chester
Julie Chichlowski
Lori Cicero
Victoria T. Clarke

Kristen Claxon
Aubrey Coggins
Amy Marty Conrad
Sara Dale
Vanessa Davis
Joan DeGregory
Ashlyn DelPriore
Rachel Denler
Deb Deverell
Gretchen Hickisch Dewey
Laura Dietrich
Kim Dion
Laura Dirks
Kayla Dreyer
Winnie DuBois
Christine Dupont-Patz
Peter Duray-Bito
Drew Elsey
Nanette Erkman
Gary Erlewine
Dagni Falvey
Caroline Faraino
Erica Faulhaber
Sue Figg
Ellen Fisher
Melinda Fisher
Mary-Katherine Fleming
Celeste Flores
Judy Foley
Brandon Foster
Ashley Foy
Tonya Frank
Justin Frodella
Katherine Fulford
Jill Gallie
Don Gallo
Jessica Gardner
Gary Geare
Alicia George
Hazel Gibson
Lynn Glassman
Stephanie Gordon
Anne Graham
Deann Gray

Jennifer Greer
Linda Griffin
Nancy Groenert
Cindy Grubenhoff
Paulette Guion
Missy Guion
Connie Hambrook
Ginger Hamilton
Kali Handford
Vicki L. Harimon
Katie Harmon
Sandra Hazzard
Nora Heitmann
Nancy M. Henderson
Beverlee Henry
Katie Henry
James Speed Hensinger
Bonnie Hill
Haley Hill
Susan Hills
Janice Hinds
Arlene Hirschfeld
Clarissa Hobson
Gabrielle Holbrook
Therese Hollek
Cathy Hollis
Diana Hotchkiss
Julie Hubbard
Susan Hunter
Michelle Ingle
Nancy Armstrong Jeffery
Virginia Jenkins
Allison Mendes Johnson
Liz Johnson
Courtney Jones
Ali Kaiser
Lark W. Katchur
Ashley Keski
Minh Dang Khoa
Taylor Kitchin
Jessica Knauf
Sally Kneser
Jennifer Knollenberg
Amanda (Cashman) Kohn

Lisa Korner
Michelle McMahon Kubota
Ruth Larson
Beverly Laughlin
Susie Law
Jane Lee
Reedy Lee
Ashley Legler
Mary Lester
Joan Loomis
Kathryn Lovell
Wendy Cutler Lowe
Constance "Stanzi" Lucy
Allison Maddox
Jack Maddox
Laurie Bruce Maddox
Molly Malone
Janet Manning
Kathy Martz
Katie Mata
Marlene Maurer
Karen Mayo
Morgan McCabe
Sandra McCalmon
Mary Beth McErlane
Michael McErlane
Patty McErlane
Sue McGinley
Jason Medrano
Gene Megyesy
Caryne Mesquita
Mark Michalski
Marina Miller
Rachel Miller
Sandie Moery
Karen Ormond Moore
Lorna G. Moore
Beverly Morrato
Helen Ruth Mozer
Jen Munro
Anne Murlowski
Samantha Myers
Grace Nelson
Bev Newton

Diana Nicholus
Valerie O'Dowd
Mary Palmquist
Zach Patz
Suzanne Peters Payne
Tracy Pearson
Elizabeth A Peetz
Kay Pinkham
Christine Ploetner
Erika Pullen
Jordan Rahtz
Rebecca Rawling
Rachel Rea
Lee Reedy
Jessica Reilly
Lea Ann Reitzig
Jenny Rementer
Harriet Renner
Vicki Reschly
Kelly Rhoades
Jennifer Rich
Judi Richardson
Kathye Ripley
Reggie Rivers
Laura Rizzo
Carolyn Roberts
Nell Roberts
Doug Robinson
Suzanne Robinson
Stacey Rubinstein
Alexis Rudisill
Catherine Rundle
Alyssa Russo
Pamela Russo
Farris Saffa
Nilufer Saltuk
Cheryl Sanderson
Tonya Sarina
Maxine Schafer
Becky Schaub
Christine Schaub
Lori Schechter
Leslie Scherer
Kerri Schlachter

Mary Schmidlin
Linda Scott
Lisa Gamel Scott
Megan Severs
Kayla Sharp
Lynne Siegel
Casse Silva
Kristen Taylor Smith
Mary Perrot Smith
Suzanne Smolik
Erin Spradlin
Laura Stenovec
Stephanie Sterling
Jennifer Stickel
Marcia Strickland
Donna Sutherland
Stephanie Sutherland
Joan Swartz
Elizabeth Sylvan
Dorothy M. Taylor
Marilyn Shields Taylor
Sheila Thomas
Susan Tracey
Cindy Van Cise
Victoria Vernon
Barbara Vetter
Barbara Vucich
Kelly Walberg
Laurel Walk
Fallon Wallace
Claire Walter
Diane Wanty
Janet Warren
Barbara Webb
Jennifer Weinstock
Megan Whelan
Jeanne Wilde
Gretchen Wilson
Kibby Wilson
Tonia Wilson
Polly Wirtz
Liz Wolfson
Katy Word
Nancy Anne Zizic

Thank you to our Recipe Testers!

Adair Ahlers
Robin Andersen
Katy Arnold
Heather Ashour
Patricia Bainter
Molli Barker
Cathy Bauer
Kendra Beatty
Grace Bird
Teresa Blount
Alexie Blue
Stewart Braden
Leah Bradley
Mary Pat Brennan
Kristin Brownson
Meagan Burgio
Kristen Busang
Brett Cameron
Sean Cameron
Marilynn Carroll
Elizabeth Dilorenzo Chester
Lauren Coffey
Aubrey Coggins
Emily Cook
Stephanie Costa
Lauren O'Neill Crist-Fulk
Kate Cygan
Bridget D'Angelo
Wendy DeBell
Gretchen Dewey
Jennifer Doskocil
Winnie DuBois
Katherine Dunn
Christine Dupont-Patz
Allison Dyer
Kirstin Eastwood
Kimberly Ann Eckert
Holly Ellsworth
Tess Enright

Hannah Falvey
Sarah Ferguson
Lainee Flanigan
Sheona French
Megan Freyman
Jessica Gardner
Caroline Gash
Alicia George
Abby Gilbertson
Jennifer Grannas
Becky Green
Missy Guion
Paulette Guion
Connie Hambrook
Alana Hancock
Megan Hannen
Katie Harmon
Sandy Hazzard
Leah Hebert
Katie Henry
Sarah Hess
Lynda Hilferty
Elizabeth Hipp
Carolyn Hunter
Michelle Ingle
Allison Johnson
Allison Mendes Johnson
Bonnie Johnson
Chesney Johnson
Ali Kaiser
Malia Keck
Sarah Keepers
Ashley Keski
Madeline Kneyger
Barbara Knight
Jennifer Knollenberg
Amanda Kohn
Susie Law
Julia Lazure

Lauren Leonard
Kathryn Lovell
Stuart Lowden
Wendy Cutler Lowe
Rob MacKenzie
Allison Maddox
Megan Maddox
Rachel Marsh
Kendall Mauch
Aubrey McCarthy
Mary Beth McErlane
Devron McMillin
Meara Melton
Caryne Mesquita
Sharyl Midcap
Rachel Miller
Sandie Moery
LaRona Mondt
Tyler Mounsey
Caitlin Munsie
Stephanie O'Donnell
Valerie O'Dowd
Jodi Padilla
Mallorie Pascucci
Isabelle Pearson
Megan Peitzmeier
Kimberly Pendleton
Kate Percival
Johanna Philio
Ellie Phillips
Tiaja Pierre
Pam Piro
Alicia C. Raciti
Rachel Rae
Jordan Rahtz
Lea Ann Reitzig
Jenny Rementer
Colleen Reusche
Kelly Rhoades

Emilie Ricker
Nell Roberts
Carole Rollins
Rebecca Rooney
Stacey Rubinstein
Alyssa Russo
Becky Schaub
Kerri Schlachter
Linda Scott
Mackenzie Shoemaker
Jenny Simpson
Callie Skersies
Erin Slattery
Kristen Taylor Smith
Laura Stenovec
Jenn Stickel
Krista Strunc
Colette Sutley
Valerie Taron
Francine Terrelll
Lauren Tidwell
Rachel Trauscht
Alissa Twiss
Kelly Van De Wyngaerde
Darcey Vertuca
Kimberly Vestal
Chelsea Vilbert
Laurel Walk
Fallon Wallace
Kristen Warnick
Megan Westberg
Megan Whelan
Kibby Wilson
Tonia Wilson
Dee Wittmer
Nicole Yue

Event Photo Index

- Details (Koozies, Napkins, Condiment Bar):
  Grace & Gather Events
- Corn Hole and Giant Jenga: Decor by Design
- Design/Styling: Grace & Gather Events

Gatherings to Go   14-17

Red Rocks Park and Amphitheatre
  18300 W. Alameda Parkway, Morrison, Colorado 80465
  redrocksonline.com

- Vintage Truck: Worldwide Vintage Autos
- Invitation and Signage: Tasha Rae Designs
- Floral: Plum Sage Flowers
- Antiques: Karl Heintz at The Antique Exchange Co-op
- Rentals (Linens, Beverage Dispensers, Glassware,
  Plates): Event Rents
- Lounge Furniture: Yonder House
- Flatware: Yonder House
- Details (Silverware/Napkin Pockets, Vintage Radio,
  Pasta Salad Box): Grace & Gather Events
- Design/Styling: Grace & Gather Events

Home for the Holidays   242-245

Home of Becky and Brian Schaub

- Floral/Decor: Plum Sage Flowers
- Rentals (Plates, Flatware, Glassware, Linens,
  Napkins): Event Rents
- Chairs: Charming Chairs
- Design/Styling: Grace & Gather Events

Market to Table   80-83

blanc
  3150 Walnut Street, Denver, Colorado 80205
  blancdenver.com

- Floral/Decor: Plum Sage Flowers
- Invitation: Tasha Rae Designs
- Menu Boards: xowyo + co Paper and Press
- Rentals (Flatware, Plates, Gold Wine Glasses):
  Yonder House
- Rentals (Table, Chairs, Glassware): Event Rents
- Details (Napkins, Cherry Place Card Bags,
  Market Styling): Grace & Gather Events
- Design/Styling: Grace & Gather Events

Spring Awakenings   56-59

Denver Botanic Gardens
  1007 York Street, Denver, Colorado 80206
  botanicgardens.org

- Floral/Decor: Plum Sage Flowers
- Rentals (Blue Chairs, Plates, Blue and Wood Chest,
  Parfait Glasses): Yonder House
- Rentals (Small Table Linens, Flatware, Glassware,
  Bowls): Event Rents
- Invitation, Menus, Signage: Tasha Rae Designs
- Linens/Napkins (Large Table): La Tavola Fine Linen
- Details (Macaron Place Cards, Tiered Display):
  Grace & Gather Events
- Design/Styling: Grace & Gather Events

Index

For more information about where to purchase the Junior League of Denver's complete collection of award-winning cookbooks, please visit jld.org.